What the Pluck?

What the Pluck?

HERMES'S JOKE: THE IMAGE OF THE HARP IN THE CINEMA

F. Marion Redd

Clairsech House   Hillsborough, NC

Unless otherwise noted, images are from public domain internet sites.
Film screenshots were made from the author's DVD collection.

Front cover images, top to bottom: unknown Marx Bros. film, publicity
shot; screenshots from *The Angel Who Pawned Her Harp* (1954),
The Bishop's Wife (1947), *In The Good Old Summertime* (1947),
Strike Up the Band (1940)
Cover designed by Russ Covey with BW&A Books
Text designed and typeset by Julie Allred, BW&A Books, Inc.

ISBN: 978-0-578-28842-0
Library of Congress Control Number: 2022907286

First edition

Dedicated to those chapter members of the American Harp Society
who always thought they were operating under the blessings
of Apollo but couldn't understand why there was
always so much inanity and dissonance.
Hermes the Trickster strikes again!

I would like to express my appreciation to the following individuals for the encouragement and inspiration that made this project happen: Elizabeth Clark, my harp fairy godmother; to my friends David Ice, Todd Walton, and Cy Esty, Jr., for their technical advice; to Norwood Pratt, whose endless supply of lychee nuts, bottomless teapot, and inspiring view of San Francisco Bay kept me grounded; and finally to my mother, Jane Barber Redd, whose haunting presence enabled me to complete this project.

CONTENTS

ILLUSTRATIONS

FOREWORD
David M. Ice

I was pleasantly surprised (and a little bit shocked!) when F. Marion Redd asked me to pen a foreword to his tome, *What the Pluck? Hermes's Joke: The Image of the Harp in the Cinema*. Being that I am neither an academic or a published author, I jumped at the chance to be in print (other than those horrid Wanted posters and awful mug shots at the post office—but that's another story!). And, as *The Far Side* cartoonist Gary Larson commented when asked by the University of Chicago if they could name a newly discovered genus of louse (found only on owls) after him: "I considered this an extreme honor. Besides, I knew no one was going to write and ask to name a new species of swan after me. You have to grab these opportunities when they come along."

Perhaps a few words about me would be in order. I am by trade a film editor; specifically, a sound editor. I have hundreds of hours of TV shows to my credit (including the last six years of *M*A*S*H*) and about sixty-five feature film credits. And weirdly, I am perhaps the only film editor who is also a professional harpist.

My cutting room at Twentieth Century Fox was literally right next door to the scoring stage, and I was able to meet, observe, and learn all about film music from the very best musicians and composers in Hollywood. Being able to chat with John Williams, Alex North, and Dominic Frontiere, among others, was one of the highlights of my life.

So I am primarily a technician as opposed to an artiste. The exigencies of film production—and orchestral rehearsal schedules—precluded deep philosophical thought or analysis. Yes, there was creativity involved in sound editing, but it was always confined by budget and time.

Ditto orchestral gigs; I would have loved to have the time to research a piece or dive into detailed study of the inner workings of orchestration. But usually, I was limited to simply getting the notes out correctly and in rhythm! My day-to-day analytical and scholarly thought was mostly restricted to *"What on earth were they thinking?"*

That said, I was always fascinated how, in film, the entire world readily accepted the notion of "suspension of disbelief." Is there an audience member anywhere who sits in a cinema and complains, "this is nothing more than an optical enlargement of grains of silver halide designed to fool the brain through persistence of vision?" No—since the dawn of cinema people willingly throw logic out the window and embrace the nonreality of what they are seeing, especially animation. The death of Bambi's mother traumatized generations of kids and it's just flat artwork! And similarly with music: a sign at a German opera house states, "God gave us music so we could pray without words." Certain pieces of music still move me to tears, for reasons I can't quite fathom or logically dissect.

So delving into this wonderful analysis of spirituality, history, mythology, science, mathematics, and musicality has been a wonderful and enlightening adventure for me. Mr. Redd manages to draw a straight line from the most ancient Egyptian deities to Hermes to the Bible's King David to—Cary Grant?! Yes! And it all makes sense!

There are many more parallels Mr. Redd illustrates that really resonated with me, both as a film technician and a working musician. I can totally relate to his descriptions of Harpo Marx's visible transition from slapstick comedian to serious musician when he plays the harp. And like many of the filmic examples Mr. Redd references, I've experienced reactions like those depicted in Disney's *The Aristocats*. I once played a wedding, and later one of the groomsmen came up to me and declared, "Dude! You nearly put me to sleep!" I didn't quite know how to react, but he quickly added, "We were all so uptight and tense—and then you started playing. And we all went 'ahhh' and relaxed!" Truly, harp music hath charms to soothe the savage beasts.

I also found it fascinating how the harp has taken many 180-degree turns over the centuries. Where it once led armies into battle (and women were forbidden to touch it!), it became feminized. I've been the recipient of several arched eyebrows and the comment "A male harpist?" I'm glad to say that, since this new millennium has dawned, more and more boys and men have taken up the harp for serious study. Many recent international competition winners have been men, and several major orchestral chairs and opera orchestra positions are now held by men. I once asked a young man why he started playing the harp. "Well, the cutest girls were in harp class! But I discovered I really, really loved the instrument."

It's amazing how, in ages past, harpists were considered to be indispensable in royal courts and by people of enormous prestige—and now many a harp major has had to face anxious parents who plead "but honey, can you make a living playing that thing?" And it stunned me to read how Timotheus (in 200 AD) was banned for the effrontery of playing a harp with eleven strings instead of the customary seven: music that "corrupted the ears of our youth . . . and the strangeness of his melody has given to our music an effeminate and artificial dress instead of the plain and orderly one." This is almost verbatim what my parents said when they saw The Beatles' 1964 debut on *The Ed Sullivan Show*. I'm not kidding. Who knew the harp could be such a "kick-ass" instrument?

Returning to the realm of film, I personally have been amazed at how the harp has been used in underscore, often against type, to subconsciously unnerve or frighten an audience. Cary Grant or Clifton Webb's angelic personas notwithstanding, composers like Bernard Herrmann, John Williams, Dominic Frontiere, and others have cleverly and deviously used the tones of the harp to scare the wadding out of us. Herrmann's last score, *Taxi Driver*, uses brittle harp glissandos to symbolize Travis Bickle's splintering sanity, culminating in perhaps the most terrifying scoring ever of a murder sequence, using brass chords, tympani, and psychotic harp glissandos. John Williams used harp as the leitmotif for the shark in *Jaws II*, and by the end of that movie, the audience was terrified any time they heard a harp!

Similarly, the psychological use of harp tonality was used to great subconscious and subliminal effect in foreign films like *Bad Education* or *Perfume: The Story of a Murderer*.

Bad Education, a 2004 film by acclaimed Spanish director Pedro Almodóvar with a brilliant score by Alberto Iglesias, is a complex murder mystery that can perhaps be summarized as a homoerotic *Vertigo* of kaleidoscopic complexity. Are we seeing a movie? Or are we seeing a movie scene being filmed? Or is this the reality behind the movie being filmed? And further, major characters are played by two different actors, and the lead actors sometimes portray two different people! On repeated viewing I finally realized that the *real* world, as opposed to the *reel* world, was indicated by a subtle change of screen aspect ratio as well as the bass wire strings on the harp. For the "movie" the harp is in a major key; but "reality" is in a minor key—as murder is truly deadly in "reality"!

In the case of *Perfume: The Story of a Murderer* (2006), directed by German director Tom Twyker—and scored by Twyker, Johnny Kilmek, and Reinhold Heil, one of the few feature films scored by its director—the harp is again used subliminally to tell the story. The music had to convey much more than the usual underscore. The key sequence in the film was over nine minutes in length that had only two significant lines of dialogue: "This man is innocent!" and "He's an *angel*!" No less a director than Stanley Kubrick decreed that this scene was unfilmable. How do you film a scene about a *smell*, a *scent*? How do you show thousands of people transform from a bloodthirsty, murderous mob into awestruck piety and total religious devotion with only two lines of dialogue over nine minutes? Twyker invoked the magic of the harp to accomplish this. The perfume is represented by "perfect" harp arpeggios, as both the scent and a linear harp arpeggio are representative of perfection. The antihero, the serial killer Grenouille, is represented by "broken" harp arpeggios (nonlinear), as he is himself "broken" mentally and morally. And earlier in the film, the murders are represented by harp harmonics, which are difficult to produce on the harp and require precise placement of the harpist's palm at exactly one-half of the length of the string to produce a harmonic's bell-like tone. Fitting, because the victims are cut down halfway through their lives!

The finished scene is brilliantly effective—nine minutes, two lines of dialogue, and the brilliant use of harp to convey the evil of Grenouille—and, as Mr. Redd has demonstrated to us, Grenouille as the "trickster" Hermes. Grenouille manages to convince thousands of angry people, even the Catholic bishop, that he is an angel! And the agent of that filmic "trick" is the harp. Wow!

I realize I have prattled on far, far too long, but I would like to close with a true story from my own Hollywood experience, which I feel validates and illustrates Mr. Redd's hypothesis.

In 1983, I was the supervising sound editor on the feature film *Two of a Kind*, directed by John Herzfeld. One of my jobs was to create unique sound effects when needed, and this film had several sequences that took place in heaven.

It is always a challenge to create a special sound for something that nobody has experienced or knows. (Did anybody really know what the transporter on *Star Trek* sounds like when it malfunctions until a sound editor created it out of a witch's brew of utterly unrelated sound effect elements?) Such was my dilemma for *Two of a Kind*. The director was visibly nervous about the "heaven background" and I knew that was going to be the first thing played when we started dubbing the picture. Nailing the first reel is vital if you're going to keep your sanity intact when doing final dubbing with a nervous director!

The day before we started dubbing, I still hadn't come up with that "heaven background." Then I realized that I had the perfect solution. There is an Aeolian harp effect that gigging harpists know about, when a stiff breeze blows through the strings of a harp and creates an eerie, floating ethereal sound that is virtually unlike anything else you can create acoustically. I decided to take my harp to the middle of the Fox parking lot on a Sunday, which was the largest and most isolated place I could think of on short notice. I set the pedals to create a harmonic chord and prayed for a good breeze from the nearby Pacific Ocean.

Hermes must have taken pity on me, for a great breeze did materialize. I popped a microphone inside the shell of the harp and recorded a good twenty minutes of Aeolian harp tonalities, changing the pedals every thirty seconds or so to obtain different tonalities and chords. I took the tape to the sound department, had it transferred to 35mm magnetic film, and created the dubbing elements for the next day.

Monday morning came, and the first thing the director wanted to hear was my heaven background. We put the reel up, and he was stunned.

"What is that sound?"

"It's the heaven background."

"But what is it?"

"The background for the heaven scenes."

"I know that, but *what is that sound? Where did you get it??*"

I just smiled and said, "I went on location, and recorded it."

Technically that was true. I never did tell him what I had done. I just smiled innocently—and the director had to agree that was the sound of heaven.

So—as Mr. Redd proposes, Hermes the Trickster struck again! And the male harpist won the battle, and the audiences accepted the suspension of disbelief and once again unknowingly embraced the harp as mythic, spiritual, and (at least to me) comedic! Who knew?!

David M. Ice retired to Glendale, Arizona, with his four dachshunds, a gigantic editing computer, two harps, and huge backlog of DVDs to peruse. He is the winner of a Motion Picture Sound Editors Golden Reel Award for his work on *M*A*S*H* and has also received Emmy and Oscar nominations for his film work. He has been active in the American Harp Society for over forty years and served as chapter president of the Phoenix chapter for nearly ten years. He has presented his lecture "Hooray for Harpywood" about Hollywood harp scoring around the world for various harp gatherings and has published about twenty-five harp arrangements. He sincerely hopes that, when he finally arrives in heaven, he will no longer have to practice.

INTRODUCTION

I n talking with friends—that is, my middle-aged friends—about the subtitle of this book, "The Image of the Harp in the Cinema," the image that comes to most of their minds, usually with a few snickers, is Harpo Marx. The assumption is that I'm doing a fluff piece on comedy. After all, the Marx Brothers are pretty airy. On a much more serious level, however, Harpo Marx is the perfect embodiment of the subtext of this study, "Hermes's instrument." Harpo is the contemporary incarnation of the "trickster," which is one of the primary attributes of the archetype of the ancient god Hermes, inventor of the lyre.

I have been a student of the harp, as of cinema, for most of my adult life and have always been interested in how the image of this instrument has been used in films for purposes beyond its orchestral qualities. For various reasons, a harp is a powerful visual cue and shows up in numerous films in the most peculiar ways perceived either consciously or unconsciously by the audience. It is my belief that a harp—unlike a piano, a violin, or a banjo—is loaded with an accumulation of cultural information and as such has become a potent symbol that points beyond itself to an archetypal image. As Carl Jung said, "The archetypes are, so to speak, organs of the pre-rational psyche" (Jacobi 46). Jung's theories of the archetype follow the same reasoning as Plato's "Ideas." Jung says, "We must presume them (the archetypes) to be the hidden organizers of representations; they are the primordial pattern underlying the *invisible order* of the unconscious psyche; down through the millennia their irresistible power has shaped and reshaped the eternal meaning of the contents that have fallen into the unconscious, and so kept them alive" (Jacobi 52).

The analogy between Plato's theory of forms and motion pictures is well known. The cinema is our contemporary Platonic cave, as Geoffrey Hill has pointed out, "the first slide projector, called the magic lantern, hints of its numinous characteristic of being able to project illuminated brilliant images onto a screen in a dark room, and thus into the human soul. Film is an excellent medium for conveying myth, whether intentionally or not" (Hill 15).

One clue to the harp's fascinating power can be found in its mythological origins. Be it fact or legend, history has given to the "Egyptian priest," Hermes, the credit for the invention of the lyre, which is known as the ancestor of the harp (Clark 4). Thoth was assimilated into the ancient Greek pantheon as Hermes and later by the Romans as Mercury, the messenger of the gods. In addition to his musical inventiveness, Hermes was known as the trickster, the god of wayfarers, merchants, and thieves and the guide of souls to the underworld. He also retained his Egyptian heritage as the patron of language and communication, as Thoth was known as the god of speech and quick wit. Both Hermes and Apollo were associated with the Greek passion for harmony and proportion. This passion was the basis of the Pythagorean school of numbers and mathematics, which ultimately laid the foundation of Western music theory.

The harp's connection to the archetype of Hermes is a major component of its power on screen. That is the foundational basis behind the trickster character of Harpo Marx, for example. Films by the Marx Brothers slow into a state of beatitude when Harpo plucks the strings of the harp. His very character is transformed while he is performing. Why? If form follows function, then the harp embodies the soul of music. It evokes a sense of transcendence unlike any other musical instrument and its effect can be seen on audience and performer alike.

Hermes's reputation as the "guide of souls" and the harp's association as the "heavenly instrument" became incorporated into Christian mythology and iconography. In the Old Testament, David praised the Lord with the harp of ten strings and in the New Testament, the saints praised God with golden harps in the Book of Revelation. That harps have become associated with angels can be seen in films like *The Bishop's Wife* and *Heaven Can Wait*.

Once this Hermetic subtext is explicated, subsequent chapters will focus on the following motifs that the harp embodies in cinema: "The Heavenly Instrument," "Transcendence," "The Bardic and Oracular Tradition," "The Naked Piano" (courtship, sexuality, and gender), "Comedy and Fantasy," and "Civilization and Culture."

If cinema is the contemporary Platonic cave and the harp has an accumulated wealth of symbolic, mythological, psychological, and sociological associations, we have a powerful archetypal situation. Whether it is experienced consciously or unconsciously, when the harp appears on the screen the presence of Hermes is once again evoked, and we are magically connected to archetypal levels of being.

ESSENCE OF THE ANCIENT

Music is an expression of the spiritual and emotional powers
of man through forms created by the architectonics of intellect.
It does not exist in pages of musical notation, nor even in
musical instruments. Music comes to life for brief moments
during performance and then like a veiled queen, is perceived
no more.

—Nicholas Bessaraboff, *Ancient European Musical Instruments,*
    1941

In the Marx Brothers comedy film *A Day at the Races*, there is a famous scene wherein Harpo Marx's character is attempting to slip away from pursuing police officers and hides in an orchestra by seating himself at a grand piano. He then proceeds to hammer out Rachmaninov's most familiar concerto with such force that the piano begins to fall apart. It finally collapses with the keyboard flying to pieces. Harpo then bends down and lifts up the piano frame from within the case and begins to play a harp solo on the strings of the piano "harp" (Figs. 1.1–1.6).

The emergence of the harp has a twofold effect in this scene. The first is a humorous retelling of the old musical axiom that "a piano is just a coffin with a harp inside it and a harp is just a naked piano." The second and more profound effect is the change in Harpo's countenance as he segues into the harp performance. As he begins to play his expression changes; his deeper, more sensitive self emerges, as if he has entered another world beyond the film.

The harp, as this scene illustrates, is more than a naked piano: it is the embodiment of the soul of music, and it is the agent of transformation.

As Melville Clark has written:

The reason that the harp has been beloved through the ages is that its tone quality is absolutely pure. Just as sunlight will penetrate where artificial light will not, the tone of the harp will cut through the orchestra because of this very distinctiveness and purity. It is surprising to

Screenshots from *A Day at the Races*, MGM, 1937

Clockwise from top left:

1.1. Harpo Marx at the piano.

1.2. Harpo playing the piano as it explodes.

1.3. Harpo picks up the piano "harp" frame,

1.4. and continues to play the strings.

1.5. Amazingly, the frame becomes a harp. 1.6. Harpo performs a harp solo before escaping.

learn that the harp tone has lived through three thousand years without change of quality. It has been improved, however, in power by modern acousticians and inventions, but it is easily seen that the tone produced from the gut string, vibrated with the human finger, flesh to flesh, vibrated on the wooden soundboard and in the air, has not been changed over thousands of years. (Clark 99)

The 1948 version of Disney's *Fantasia* was a study in the relationship between sound and animation images. The film began with an exploration of the soundtrack. Sounds of the studio orchestra directed by Leopold Stokowski (who is listed in the credits as the only human actor) were given visual images. The first example, naturally, was of the harp. The clear tones of the harp playing a glissando fading away were represented like ripples in a pool, rounded like waves of water rippling outward. It was a clear image of harmonious movement moving across the screen. Other instrument examples displayed different sound patterns, but the harp was the pinnacle of harmonious vibration.

If form follows function, then it may be said the harp embodies the "soul of music." Its very design with one string for one note is a visual depiction of the musical scale with all its mathematical divisions. Only the pipe organ displays the musical scale in a similar visible fashion with its various ranks of pipes organized in upward curves of descending pitch. The gentle curve of the organ scale clearly demonstrates the Pythagorean concept of the division of a tone into its relative parts. It would be physically impossible, however, to reach all the strings of the same scale if the harp were strung with the soundboard exactly perpendicular to the string. Thus, the soundboard is rotated, closing the angle between it and the strings. This arrangement forms the classic triangular shape of the modern concert harp by compressing the scale into the acute curvaceous form known as the "harmonic curve." This is the single most distinguishing characteristic the harp has acquired since medieval times.

Unlike the harp, the organ is isolated from the source of musical vibrations represented by the pipes as with the piano and harpsichord. A keyboard is interposed between the musician and the instrument rather like an impenetrable barrier that separates the lover and the beloved from the material and immaterial realms. As keyboard instruments are more visually literal in representation of the scale, so are other instruments necessarily more abstract and abbreviated. The violin or guitar is a stringed abstraction relying on the fingerboard or frets to supply the required tones from only a few strings. That is, the production of tone from these instruments may also appear somewhat mysterious—pulling so many notes or chords from so few strings. With the harp, by contrast, the miracle of a complete scale with resonant overtones is visible. Thus, in the guise of slapstick, Harpo releases the imprisoned soul of music from the piano with his transforming harp solo.

This elemental quality of the harp as described by Melville Clark is related to the instrument's primitive beginnings. As Richard Hayward, author of *The Story of the Irish Harp*, says, "The word *HARP* is derived from the Scandinavian *HARPA*, and the Anglo-Saxon *HEARPE*, and these words come from the root *HARPAN*, to pluck, which in turn is derived from the old Aryan root *RAP*, to seize or clutch" (Hayward 4). The musical tones produced by the strings diminish rapidly. They are like stones thrown into a pool of water that cause ripples to fan out across the surface. A result of this action is that the harp is unable to produce sustained notes like the flute, organ, or violin. Since the music of the harp seems to be coaxed from the air by the caress of the harpist, it came to be identified with the wind deities. It was logically associated with angels as a contributing link between Heaven and Earth.[1]

It is unclear to scholars when musical instruments were invented. It is thought rather that they evolved. Curt Sachs says that "no early instrument was 'invented,' if we conceive of invention as the ultimate bringing into being of an idea long contemplated and experimented with. The supposition of such a process commits the current fallacy of superimposing modern reasoning upon early man. Actually, he was quite unaware, as he stamped on the ground or slapped his body, that his actions were the seeds of the earliest instruments" (Sachs 25). The question of which instruments probably came into being first cannot be answered until a more basic problem is solved: what impulses in humankind resulted in the development of musical instruments? All higher creatures express emotion by motion. But humankind alone, apparently, can regulate and coordinate their emotional movements; humans alone are gifted with conscious rhythm (Sachs 26).

Musical instruments are as old as mankind itself. They must have existed before any awareness of tonality or attempt to reproduce a particular melody (Buchner 6). According to music historian Karl Geiringer,

1.7. *"Can't you think of something to do with that silly harp?"* John Ruge cartoon, *Playboy* magazine, ca. 1960s

The function of music in prehistoric times was quite different from what it came to be in later periods. Music was not made to provide pleasure and aesthetic enjoyment. Its purpose was to help man in his struggle against overwhelming forces of nature (Fig. 1.7). For primitive man musical sound, whose origin he did not quite understand, had a mysterious quality, and he attributed magical effects to it. Played at funeral services, it was intended to assure rebirth. Strong taboos were often attached to musical instruments and dire punishment threatened the unauthorized who dared to use or even touch them. (Geiringer 29)

There is archaeological evidence of the magical functions of early musical instruments. The famous Stone Age painting in the Cave of the Trois-Frères shows a kind of flute played by a masked dancer who is wrapped in the skin of a wild beast, which turns him into a diabolical figure. From these supernatural implications musical instruments have never been wholly freed. Despite the ever-growing importance of the aesthetic aspects of sound, brought about by technical improvements, the symbolic values of the instruments have continued to carry weight up to the very threshold of the present age (Geiringer 30).

The first musical instruments have not survived. They were destroyed shortly after being placed beside a dead person in his grave, or they may have been thrown away. The history of music, therefore, in trying to trace the rise of musical instruments, must base all its theories upon scanty finds of prehistoric objects and upon the study of various types of instruments found today among primitive peoples whose musical culture is thought, at present, to be on the same level as that of early humankind (Buchner 10). The association of musical instruments with death provides a mixed blessing. While most artifacts did not survive the grave, the most significant discoveries came from tombs in the arid Middle East. Specimens of ancient box lyres and angle harps have been recovered in Egypt and Mesopotamia. The paintings in the tomb of Ramesses III

(c. 1200–1168 BC) in the Valley of the Kings at Thebes provide the most remarkable evidence of the most advanced harps of the time. The remains of a *cruit* or *chrotta*, which emerged from the Dark Ages as a type of rectangular descendant of the *kithara*, was discovered in the remains of the seventh-century burial ship at Sutton Hoo in Suffolk, England.

In the *Annals of the New York Academy of Sciences*, author David Huron writes that there is strong support for the theory that music was an evolutionary adaptation. In his article "Is Music an Evolutionary Adaptation?" he writes: "Complex evolutionary adaptations arise only over many millennia. Accordingly, for a behavior to be adaptive, it must be very old. As we have seen, music-making does indeed conform to the criterion of great antiquity." He goes on to say that "the neurological evidence is at least consistent with the possibility that there are specialized music-related brain structures. In order for a behavior to be adaptive, the behavior itself must enhance the propagation of the individual's genes. Musical behaviors are consistent with mood modification and group mood synchronization—and these synchronous states are at times clearly associated with situations where group efforts are adaptive" (Huron 59).

Musicologists classify the harp as a chordophone.[2] It is a direct descendant of the first primitive instruments developed by humans. All musical instruments can be traced back to four types of devices that actually generate sound: (1) vibrating strings (stringed instruments or chordophones); (2) vibrating air columns (wind instruments or aerophones); (3) vibrating membranes, as in drums with skin heads (membranophones); (4) matter vibrating without aid of strings, air, or membranes (idiophones) such as slit drums, bells, gongs, chimes, and xylophones (Stunzi 40).

Chordophonic instruments or chordophones have a string or set of strings as a primary vibrator. The word "chordophone" is derived from two Greek words, *cordon*, string (specifically, gut-string), and *fone*, sound; therefore, chordophone means a "string-sounder" (Bessaraboff 207). Chordophones with their plucked, struck, and bowed strings are usually subdivided into four general groups: lyres, lutes, zithers, and harps. Lyres, the first group, have strings that run parallel to the soundboard and continue beyond it to a crossbar or yoke held by two arms projecting from the soundbox. The ancient Greek *lyra* was a bowl lyre with the soundboard of skin stretched over a shallow bowl made of wood or the back of a turtle shell. The ancient Greek *kithara* used a box made of wooden front, back, and side walls joined together. While the *lyra* was always light and unadorned, the *kithara* had a massive and often richly ornamented body (Fig. 1.8). Harps are instruments whose strings, invariably plucked, do not run parallel to the soundboard, but vertically away from it (Fig. 1.9). Lutes, in the general sense of the term, have a soundbox terminating in a neck, which serves both as a handle and as a device for extending the strings beyond the soundbox. This category includes plucked lutes and bowed lutes such as violins and viols, etc. Zithers

1.8. Lyre/*cithara* player on vase

1.9. Painted wooden figure of a girl playing a harp, New Kingdom after 1200 BC, postcard, British Museum

1.10. Sacred harp player, Cycladic third millennium BC, postcard, Metropolitan Museum of Art

have neither neck nor yoke; the strings are stretched between the two ends of a body that may be a shallow box, a tube, or a stick equipped an additional resonator such as gourds (Stunzi 40). One of the earliest depictions of musical instruments ever found is a fragment of a marble figure excavated in Babylonia dating from the third to fourth millennium BC on which a musician is represented playing a harp (Fig. 1.10).

The evolution from prehistoric and primitive civilizations to modern-day civilization involves a corresponding evolution from folk and ritual instruments to instruments intended for entertainment and art. The division of labor and class distinctions in urban culture results in the formation of a professional class of singers and musicians. It is no more the "people" that play and sing for magic, devotional, and social purposes, but a distinct class, or even a caste, of musicians (Sach 67). In ancient Assyria musicians were given privileged positions and ranked above the court officials, immediately below the gods and the king. The voices of the gods were often compared with the sound of musical instruments (Buchner 12).

Examples of both the lyre and the harp can be found in sculpture and paintings in ancient Mesopotamia and Egypt. It is thought that the lyre preceded the development of the harp. In Egypt, however, the lyre did not appear until eight hundred years after it was known in Sumer. The Old Kingdom (2900-2475 BC) did not have one instrument that did not exist in Sumer simultaneously. Contact between the two nations must have come to an end before 2700 BC as the

1.11. Egyptian lyre player

lyre had an outstanding role in Sumerian ceremonies about that time, although it was still unknown in Egypt. It was nearly eight hundred years before an Egyptian painter depicted a passage of Semitic nomads coming down to Egypt with their families and belongings, and among them a man playing the lyre—the first recorded in the vicinity of the Nile (Sachs 86).

At this point, history blurs as there were sudden changes in the Middle East. There was a violent invasion of peoples from Central Asia, probably caused by sudden change in climate; the Kassites conquered Mesopotamia and put an end to the Babylonian empire; Abraham, the patriarch of Israel, is said to have migrated from Ur in Chaldea to Canaan; the nomadic Hyksos entered Egypt and destroyed the civilization of the Middle Kingdom (Sachs 86). This was when lyres came to Egypt from the north. It was not until the reign of Thutmose III (1501-1447 BC) in the Eighteenth Dynasty, after the Hyksos invasions and subsequent wars in Palestine, Phoenicia, and Syria, that Egyptian musical tradition was broken and the lyre, lute, and frame drum travelled south in the wake of the girl slave trade (Fig. 1.11) (Marcuse 361).

Sibyl Marcuse suggests that the lyre proceeded from Mesopotamia west through Syria and Palestine into Egypt. The main source of knowledge of the music of the ancient Hebrews is in the Bible and Talmudic commentaries. Among the instruments of the Hebrews' nomadic period was the *kinnor*, related to the Egyptian word *knr*, which was identified as a box lyre. This was the "harp" of King David. Hebrew coins struck during the second century BC portray lyres with as many as seven strings (Marcuse 361). "It is interesting," says Roger Bragard, "that the hieroglyphic writing *knr*, with which the Egyptians designated the lyre, is related to the word *kinnor*, a kind of lyre said to have been invented by the Phoenicians and widely known to the Syrians and the Hebrews. As the *kinnor* was used in the rites of Astarte, it is hardly surprising to find it subject to the maledictions of the Prophets, such as Isiah and Ezekiel"

1.12. Large standing
Egyptian arched harp

(Bragard 31). "The melodies that the *kinnor* played or accompanied were gay
and unsuited to sorrow; the Jews refused to play that instrument during the
Babylonian Exile. They suspended their *kinnorim* on the willows; 'how should
they sing the Lord's song in a strange land?' When the prophets admonished the
people, they threatened that the *kinnor*, symbol of joy and happiness, would be
silenced unless the people desisted from sin. Instruments still were bound to
well-defined occasions and moods" (Sach 108).

The arched harp made its appearance in the ancient Near East in Sumer.
The first arched harps were much like a large, curved bow. These were later
followed by angled harps. Both were held with the soundbox vertical with the
string arm down—exactly upside down from the modern position of the instrument. It could be that the musicians thought that the sound was projected
better if the resonating chamber were away from the player's body. As harps
became increasingly larger and gravity became a part of the equation, the position was switched, and the more familiar posture was adopted with the soundbox resting against the player with the string arm above.

The Egyptian arched harp, now considered to be descended from that of
Sumer, first appears in the Fourth Dynasty (2723-2463 BC). According to
Professor Roger Bragard, "It was in Egypt, after 2500 BC, that the most rapid
development of the harp took place" (Bragard 31). Curt Sachs writes that "the
harp depicted on many reliefs was indeed the most highly prized instrument of
Egypt" (Fig. 1.12) (Sachs 92). At first it was still in arched form, as in Mesopotamia, but soon the angular harp made its appearance, and from then on there
was a degree of discrimination between the status of the two instruments;
the arched harp was gradually abandoned to be played only by mendicants,
whereas the popularity of the angular harp—whose strings now totaled ten—
spread among the leisured classes and the nobility and finally established itself
at the pharaoh's court.[3] Very large harps, with anthropomorphic bases, appear

in pictures painted in the tombs of Ramesses III, who reigned from about 1200 to 1168 BC (Bragard 31).

These harps, which were over seven feet high, lacked a column or forepillar, an important part of the modern harp (Fig. 1.12). Since it is the column that completes the triangle and strengthens the harp frame, it is supposed that with a large column, less harps were tuned in a rather low pitch as they would have been unable to withstand the tension of higher-tuned strings (Rensch 4). In the Old Kingdom, the harp was exclusively played by men. Sachs writes that later on women became harpists as well, but they played the shoulder and footed harp mostly (Sach 94).

Theories of how the lyre and the harp reached Greece vary among various historians.[4] According to Roger Bragard, it was under the New Empire (1580-1090 BC) that the lyre was introduced to Europe (from Egypt) through Asia Minor and established itself there (Bragard 31). The lyre, closely related to the *phorminx*, *chelys*, and *barbitos* (all later variations of the lyre concept), might have been introduced to Greece from the Balkan peninsula (Geiringer 34).

The *kithara* was probably imported from Asia Minor via the islands of the Aegean and the harp was reintroduced from the orient. Geiringer claims that harps (with strings perpendicular to the soundboard, not parallel as in a lyre) had been used in prehistoric Greece but had disappeared. A different type of the instrument was introduced from the orient about the middle of the fifth century BC. In this harp, known as a *psalterion*, *magadis*, or *trigonon*, the neck is attached to the body at right angles (Fig. 1.13). On account of its light and delicate tone, the harp was the favorite instrument of Greek women, but it never achieved the popularity of the lyre or *kithara* (Geiringer 36).

Like earlier civilizations, Greek mythology emphasized the magical power of music. Orpheus, the divine musician, could not only tame wild beasts with the sound of his lyre, but his song moved the spirits of the underworld and he was allowed to bring his dead wife back to life. Here the archaic belief that music miraculously bridges the gap between death and life is still in evidence. Music was also reputed to have the gift of magically influencing nature and healing sickness. Asklepios, the god of medicine, was known as the son of Apollo, the god of art and song (Geiringer 32).

In sharp contrast to the fine arts, apparently Greek music was almost entirely imported. The Phrygian and Lydian tonalities were attributed to Asia Minor. "No instrument originated in Greece," the geographer Strabo writes: "One writer says, 'striking the Asiatic *cithara*'; another calls the *auloi* 'Berecyntian' and 'Phrygian'; and some of the instruments have been called by barbarian names, *nablas*, *sambyke*, *barbitos*, *magadis*, and several others" (Sachs 128).

Greek music gave rise to the doctrine of *ethos*, which was highly elaborated by Pythagoras, Plato, and Aristotle. These philosophers emphasized the great educational value of music. They contended that it was beneficial for young

1.13. Greek woman playing *trigonon*, mid-fifth century BC, vase painting

1.14. Etruscan lyre player, Tarquinia dei Leopardi, postcard, Italy

people to hear melodies based on the right kind of scales and rhythmic patterns and accompanied by carefully chosen instruments (Fig. 1.14). On the other hand, they held that acquaintance with the wrong kind of music might lead to intemperance and moral turpitude. From the beginning it was felt, both in Sparta and in Athens, that laws had to govern the nature of music, as it exercised a decisive influence on the human character (Geiringer 33). In the first century BC, Damon said that "in singing and playing the lyre a boy ought properly to reveal not only courage and moderation but also justice" (Maas 166). According to Plato, the proper subjects of an aristocratic education are letters (*grammata*), lyre playing (*kitharizein*), and wrestling (*palaiein*). Plato's ideal educational system suggested that a pupil should study literature for three years between ages ten and thirteen, and the lyre for another three years between thirteen and sixteen. The standard term for a lyre teacher is *kitharistes*. Only the schoolboy's *lyra* and the *kithara* are to be allowed in Plato's ideal state, along with the shepherd's panpipes, or *syrinx* (Fig. 1.15). Aristotle goes even further in banning instruments from the ideal community, for he disapproves not only of Plato's blacklisted instruments but also of the *kithara*, which he regards as unsuitable for educational purposes because it requires too much technical expertise (Maas 186). In Plato's view, the goal of all this training is to instill *sophrosyne* (moderation) in the young pupil; he wants the lyre teachers to concern themselves more with character development than with performance skills (Fig. 1.16) (Maas 167).

David Huron concludes in his study "Is Music an Evolutionary Adaption" that the evidence for mood regulation and synchronization is suggestive: "The emergence of the secondary or socialized emotions in child development is strongly associated with musical empathy, understanding, and sophistication. The pertinent research on child development implies a social role for music" (Huron 59).[5]

In the Pythagorean canon this emphasis of the ethos of music rested on

1.15. Greek schoolboy with music teacher, fourth century BC vase

1.16. Greek students, pottery fragment, fourth century BC

musical vibration and number. I will go into the Greek theory of harmony in greater detail in the chapter on Hermes; however, for now, for understanding the Greek preference for the lyre over the harp, some points regarding Pythagorean ideas are useful. In *Jesus Christ Sun of God: Ancient Cosmology and Early Christian Symbolism*, author David Fideler gives the following rationale for the ancients:

> As the Pythagoreans realized, the study of proportion and harmony constitutes an objective science and comprises the starting point for a philosophy of whole systems. A philosophy of whole systems is based on the premise that there is an underlying unity behind the nature of things, and that the many parts of an organism are intrinsically related to one another within the context of a greater whole. This principle of relatedness is seen to exist inherently in the structure of the human body, the biosphere, and the structure of the solar system. A philosophy of whole systems recognizes this "fitting together" and trains the mind to see how the parts relate to the whole; it helps us to think in terms of the whole; leading our minds and our conceptions to follow the path of Nature itself. In order to achieve this type of "proportional thinking," the ancient

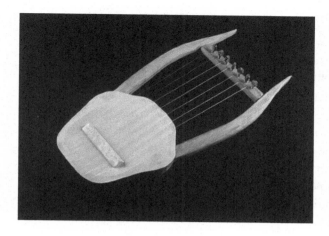

1.17. Reconstruction
of Greek lyre with
hide-covered soundbox

Pythagoreans both studied and exposed their intellects to the pure principles of geometrical and musical harmony. (Fideler 1993, 186–87)

The Greeks went about studying this unity from diversity with a curious instrument called a monochord. When a string is plucked, it first vibrates as a unit. Then, if fretted, it vibrates in two parts, in three parts, in four parts, and so on, moving toward infinity. It is also possible to hear the haunting chorus of overtones, which are produced geometrically at harmonic nodal points. The monochord demonstrates the principles of perfect harmony as innately existing in the natural order of things. The harmonic overtone series, itself reflecting the simple primacy of number, is the basis of all musical expression and contains the perfect consonances of unison (1:1), the octave (1:2), the perfect fifth (2:3), and the perfect fourth (3:4). When a single string is plucked, at first glance it seems as though you are producing a single note; but, if you listen more closely, you are led to the realization that you are really producing a *chord*, reflecting the principles of perfect harmony (Fideler 1993, 189).

This passion for harmony (as the Greeks understood it) seems to be the key in understanding why the lyre, *kithara*, and *barbitos* were the favored instruments, while the *trigonon* (triangular harp) was snubbed and outright condemned by Plato.

The tortoise shell lyra, the instrument whose invention the mythmakers assigned to the enterprising infant Hermes, serves as the stringed instrument simplest to play (Maas 202). The lyre originally consisted of a tortoiseshell with a tympanum of ox hide stretched over it, while the arms of the yoke were of antelope horns. Later the whole instrument was fashioned of wood and the strings were supported by a bridge and fixed to the crosspiece of the yoke by means of fatty hide (Fig. 1.17). By twisting this hide the instrument could be tuned. It is thought that the instrument was played both with the bare hands and with a hard plectrum (Geiringer 34). The number of strings, originally made of hemp and later of gut, was gradually increased. Up to the seventh century BC, three to five strings were generally used. In the classical period of Greek music, during the sixth and fifth centuries, seven strings were the rule. They were tuned to the notes of the pentatonic scale, with five notes (E, G, A, B, D) to the octave, omitting the semitones.

The *kithara* (Fig. 1.18), while resembling the lyre, was much more massive, was made of wood, and had up to twelve strings. It is significant to note, this increase in the number of strings met with much resistance. It is reported by Timotheus of Miletos that the authorities of conservative Sparta actually cut off four of the newly added strings of his kithara. Writing about 200 AD, the Greek rhetorician and grammarian Athenaeus related the following:

> Whereas Timotheus the musician, coming to our city, has deformed the majesty of our ancient music, and despising the lyre of seven strings, has by the introduction of a multiplicity of notes corrupted the ears of our youth, and by the number of his strings and the strangeness of his melody has given to our music an effeminate and artificial dress instead of the plain and orderly one in which it has hitherto appeared. . . . The kings and the Ephori have therefore resolved to pass censure on Timotheus for these things, and further to oblige him to cut off all the superfluous strings of his eleven, and to banish him from our domain, that men may be warned for the future not to introduce into Sparta any unbecoming customs. (Schwartz 276)

The technical differences between the lyre and the *kithara* had some influence on the employment of the two instruments. The lyre was the instrument of the dilettante and the novice, being used only to accompany singers; the *kithara*, meanwhile, was played by professionals and was a solo instrument (Fig. 1.19). The *kithara*, like the lyre, was employed mainly for the accompaniment of lyric and epic poetry (Geiringer 35).

Also clearly defined is the role of the large, ornate *kithara*, which was the chief instrument of Apollo. The close connection between the *kithara* and the god of music himself reflects the prestigious status of the instrument. In all cases, the performers are men—again a reflection of the high status of the *kithara* in a culture that restricted the role and activities of women (Maas 202).

The emotional mood to which they both gave expression was calm and restrained, and aptly described as "Apollonian" (Geiringer 35). Paintings on Greek pottery from the classical period clearly show the lyre as the instrument of the schoolboy and an important part of his education. The *kithara*, on the other hand, usually accompanies professional singers and divinities. The Spartans and Athenians, who took the greatest care in providing a balanced education for citizens and soldiers alike, were rather averse to the adoption of these instruments whose sounds they may have thought likely to weaken spiritual or

1.18. Professional *kithara* player, Greek amphora, postcard, Metropolitan Museum of Art

1.19. Reconstruction of Roman *kithara*, postcard, Museo della Civiltà Romana

1.20. Greek *barbitos* (elongated lyre)

moral strength; they preferred the lyre and the *kithara* to the extent of considering them their national instruments (Bragard 33).

Lyres were indeed the chief, divine instruments. When "the blest gods the genial day prolong, Apollon tun'd the lyre," and in the famous contest between Apollo and Marsayas, the national divinity opposed the *kithara* to the *aulos* or flute of the foreign Silenus. As Apollo's attribute, the *kithara* expressed the so-called Apollonian side of Greek soul and life—wise moderation, harmonious control, and mental equilibrium—while the pipes stood for the Dionysian side, for inebriation and ecstasy (Sachs 131). The literature and vase paintings bear witness to the well-defined roles that stringed instruments acquired within Greek social customs. The *barbitos*, the elongated tenor lyre (Fig. 1.20), functioned as the chief stringed instrument associated with Dionysus—the god himself and his attendants, the maenads and the satyrs. Not surprisingly the *barbitos* also has close associations with Eros, who sometimes appears playing the instrument himself or hovering over a group of women in the women's quarters, one of whom performs for the others (Maas 202).

Orpheus, the musician par excellence in the eyes of antiquity, has become a symbol of the decadence that Plato attributed to the class of professional virtuoso performers against whom, in his deeply ingrained conservatism, Plato felt scornful resentment (Maas 187). In the ancient Greek marriage of music and poetry, clearly music was the handmaiden to speech and singing. Plato went to the length of condemning purely instrumental music:

> Our poets divorce melody and rhythm from words, by their employment of *kithara* and *aulos* without vocal accompaniment, though it is the hardest of tasks to discover what such wordless rhythm and tune signify. . . . Nay we are driven to the conclusion that all this so popular employment of *kithara* and *aulos*, not subordinated to the control of dance or song for the display of speed or virtuosity, and the reproduction of the cries of animals, is in the worst of bad taste. (Sachs 131)

Schwartz makes the astute observation that for some strange reason it never occurred to the gifted Greeks, with their knowledge of the harmonic intervals of the musical scale, that they could make an instrument of many strings, which would have the great musical resources of modern keyboard instruments. Just think though: if such penalties were inflicted on Timotheus for increasing the number of strings of the lyre from seven to eleven, what terrible things might have happened to anyone who dared to build a clavichord, comprising two or three octaves! (Schwartz 275–76).

One not-so-obvious reason that may have kept the Greeks faithful to the seven-stringed lyre tradition is that the seven-note musical scale corresponds to the seven vowels and the seven Chaldean planets of Greco-Roman antiquity. According to Joscelyn Godwin, in a late classical work written by a certain Porphyry (not to be confused with the famous Neoplatonist), a commentary on Dionysius of Thrace states that the Greek letter alpha is consecrated to Venus, iota to the Sun, omicron to Mars, upsilon to Jupiter, and omega to Saturn. This leaves unassigned two vowels/notes (epsilon and eta) and two astrological planets (the Moon and Mercury). In addition, Eusebius of Caesarea (c. 260–340 AD) quotes the *Philosophy from Oracles* of Porphyry the Neoplatonist in which is preserved the following oracle of Apollo:

> Invoke Hermes and the Sun in the same way,
> On the Sun's day, and invoke the Moon when her day comes,
> Then Cronos and Rhea, and next Aphrodite,
> With silent prayer, invented by the greatest mage,
> King of the seven notes, known to all. (Godwin 21)

If the lyre represented the Apollonian side of Greek soul and life, then the *trigonon* (or angled harp) was considered a foreign interloper and a potential threat to the social and moral order. One is reminded of the famous line in the film *Amadeus*, when the emperor remarks on the young Mozart's new work, "There are too many notes!" Sachs says the harp was always considered an alien instrument in Greece and Rome, as coming from the Orient. Plato condemned it because the greater number of strings and notes facilitated modulation, instability, and, therewith, *hedone*—that is, sensory pleasure. The *trigonon*, being an instrument of intimacy and dreamy absorption, was played almost exclusively by women, courtesans as well as ladies of correct society (Sachs 134). The *psalterion, trigonon, magadis,* and *pektis,* as the harp was called, were of Lydian origin. The Spartan poet Alkman, a Lydian himself, was the first to mention it, in the seventh century BC. The *magadis* was played with bare fingers without the plectrum and had twenty strings, that is, ten double strings tuned in octaves. A hundred years after Alkman, Anacreon in one of his love lyrics sang:

> O Leucastis, I play
> magade of twenty strings.
> And thou art in thy youthful prime!

Anacreon also wrote:

> I have eaten the mid-day meal of honey-cakes broken fine,
> And now on the graceful harp I daintily thrum the strings,
> Making merry with song for thee, O dainty maiden mine!
>   (Sachs 134)

The *magadis* was probably a harp, since it, too, is plucked rather than struck. Since it is thought that the word *magadis* may be of Lydian origin we may wonder if the Greeks borrowed an instrument of the harp type from the Lydians (Lydia lay in coastal Asia Minor or modern Turkey), calling it sometimes by its original name, *magadis,* and sometimes by their own name, *pektis,* a term that might also describe a harp (Maas 40). If the exact nature of the *pektis* or *magadis* is uncertain, the Lydian origin of the instrument is confirmed through two fifth-century sources. Pindar says that Terpander heard the "twanging of the tall *pektis*" at banquets of the Lydians, and the historian Herodotus describes the marching of Lydian troops to the sound of *syrinx, pektis* and *aulos* (Maas 40). As noted earlier, the word *pektis* is one of the few Greek names for the harp and is derived from the verb *pegnuein,* "to fasten." There is little doubt that it was the harp, for in addition to references to plucking, there is Plato's statement that both the *pektis* and *trigonon* are many-stringed instruments in contrast to the *lyra* or *kithara* (Fig. 1.21) (Maas 148).

The *pektis* was also mentioned in the poetry of Sappho: "Sweeter-melodied by far than the *pektis,* more golden than gold." The close association of the poets of Lesbos with the instrument is further reflected in the later tradition that claimed that Sappho was its inventor (Maas 40). The term for a female harp performer is *psaltria,* literally "one who plucks" (Maas 184). The later feminine associations of the *pektis* are perhaps reflected in the Hellenistic tradition that Sappho was the first player of the instrument. In any case, nowhere in the literature of the classical period, except for Herodotus, do we find mention of the

1.21 Women playing *trigonon* (left), *phorminx* (center), and *lyre* (right), mid-fourth century BC

use of the *pektis* for military purposes; instead, it is described as a woman's instrument (Maas 148). Diogenes of Oinomaos writes of the Lydian and Bactrian maidens who worship the virgin goddess Artemis while they dance and play:

> But I hear that the Lydian and Bactrian maidens
> Living by the river Halys worship Artemis,
> the Tmolian goddess, in a laurel-shaded grove,
> Striking the *magadis* with motions responding
> To the pluckings of triangular *pektides*,
> While welcome *aulos*, in a Persian tune
> Sounds in concord for the dances. (Maas 148)

Much more than the various lyres, the *pektis* is noticeably (but not exclusively) associated with women players in Greek literature. Nevertheless, in its Lydian homeland, the instrument was evidently used in masculine contexts, particularly to provide music for military marches. Anacreon, one of the eastern Greeks through whom the *pektis* may have become known in mainland Greece, speaks of both a male dancer and a male serenader who plays the instrument (Maas 148).

The name *trigonon*, meaning "three-cornered," first appears in fragments of plays of Sophocles in the second half of the fifth century. Sophocles emphasizes the foreign nature of the instrument when he speaks of the Lydian *pektis* sounding in concord with the Phrygian *trigonon*. Information about the *trigonon* from literary sources is scanty, but what little there is makes clear that harps were considered appropriate instruments for women musicians (Maas 150).

Another comic fragment probably dating to the last quarter of the fifth century demonstrates that men also played the *trigonon*:

> It's old-fashioned to sing the songs of Stesichoros, Alkman, and
>   Simonides.
> Now it's in to listen to Gnesippos, who has fashioned
> Night-time songs for adulterers to sing to the *iambuke* and *trigonon*
> And thus to lure their ladies out. (Maas 150)

The contrast between the respectability of the old lyric poets and the dubious purposes ascribed to Gnesippos's tunes seems to suggest a low status for the accompanying instruments as well. This is confirmed in a comic fragment by Rupolis, who describes a male performer's obscene gestures in an unknown context:

> You who play the drum well
> And strum upon *trigonon*s,
> And wiggle your ass
> And stick your legs up in the air.

Given these associations, it is perhaps not surprising that the *trigonon* is specifically singled out by both Plato and Aristotle as not being suited for the ideal state they envisioned at the dawn of the Hellenistic era (Maas 151).

The term "Hellenistic" designates the period that began with Alexander the Great and ended with the conquest of the east by the Romans. According to historian Helmut Koester, the most characteristic phenomenon of this period is the intensification of the process of "Hellenization," namely the expansion of Greek language, education, and culture initiated by the establishment of Macedonian and Greek political dominion over the nations of the former Persian Empire. When Greek culture encountered Rome and fell under its political domination, the Greek element prevailed over Rome itself. Roman culture was deeply affected by Greek art, architecture, philosophy, and literature. The development of the Roman imperial period cannot be understood without Hellenism, and insofar as the Roman Empire was Hellenized, it found its natural continuation in the "Greek" Byzantine period. Indeed, Christianity, which had its beginnings in the early Roman imperial period, entered the Roman world as a Hellenistic religion, specifically as the heir to an already Hellenized Jewish religion. To some degree the Greeks became Orientalized, and many Orientals became Hellenized (Koester 42, 44). For several centuries, the Greeks retained the simplicity of form in the lyre and harp, which suited their mode of education. In the middle of the second century BC the Romans conquered Greece and thus became the immediate successors to the culture of Alexandria. Because they did not believe in the educational power of music, they therefore paid less attention to it than the Greeks. Plato's musical ethics were replaced by the formalism of Epicurus, which was most clearly formulated in Latin by Cicero. He held the very Roman view that music could not be of any real benefit to man but supplied man only with childish amusement, for it did not point the way to spiritual happiness (Buchner 15).

The Romans first took over the instruments of the Greeks without modification, no doubt, but Alexandrian times saw various modifications made to musical instruments, including the increase in the number of the *kithara*'s strings and the appearance of *kitharas* with different registers. Musicians cultivated extreme virtuosity. According to Livy, it was in 187 BC that the influence of Eastern music began affecting Rome, and Juvenal tells us that it was at this time that the *sambuca* (another word for a harp) appeared. This instrument was played by the *ambubajae* of whom Horace speaks; the women of easy virtue, of Syrian origin, who had banded together in a corporation to ply their trade (Bragard 34).

In religious rites, music was employed to ban evil spirits and to evoke ecstasy. Dirges resounded at the biers of the dead. Music was particularly important in comedy and drama, where it was employed in overtures, interludes between the acts, solos, dances, and choruses (Geiringer 39).

Sybil Marcuse writes: "In Roman times, the *kithara* [now spelled *cithara*] became heavier, rectangular in form, over-ornamented, although a simple rectangular model is occasionally depicted in the hands of women players. Neither harp nor lyre could play an important role in the musical life of as martial a people as the Romans. The Greeks constituted preponderantly a 'string audience,' as we should say today while the Romans remained primarily a 'wind audience'" (Marcuse 366). For the Romans, the most important group of musical instruments was the brass, which played a dominant role in Roman military music—the only musical field in which the Romans surpassed the Greeks (Buchner 15). "The music of imperial Rome," Buchner writes, "already showing signs of decadence, was completely under the influence of Greek musicians and Greek musical instruments, which were slowly succumbing to an ethos of megalomania" (Buchner 15). They constructed *lyrae* and *kitharae* as big as sedan chairs and liked to assemble massed orchestras and choruses. These events reached such enormous proportions that Seneca reported seeing more performers than members of the audience at the theatre. The Romans showed definite preference for wind instruments, possibly because their tone was more powerful than that of the delicate stringed instruments (Geiringer 39).

Besides the harp, the only other instrument to find its way from antiquity into post-classical times was the *hydraulos*, or "water organ," which was

1.22. Mosaic depicting a *hydraulos* (water organ), Tripoli Museo Archeologico

a featured instrument at the circus (Fig. 1.22). The *hydraulos* is traditionally ascribed to the Alexandrian physicist Ktesibios, who was born between 300 BC and 250 BC. In the *hydraulos*, the principle of the *syrinx* and the bagpipe were cleverly combined. Air was pumped into a hemispherical container standing in a cylinder of water, which kept the air under constant pressure. From this container a tube led to cross-channels furnished with flute pipes. These pipes were made to sound by means of an ingenious system of sliders operated with the help of large keys. The *hydraulos* had its heyday during the Roman Empire. According to the historian Suetonius, in addition to the *cithara*, Nero liked to play the organ. Cicero, a century before Nero, also proclaimed himself a great lover of organ music. One can imagine that the water organ probably sounded something like a modern circus calliope—shrill and loud. Also, because the *hydraulos* was an instrument capable of playing polyphonic music invented at a time when only monadic music was practiced—a situation that held good for long afterward—the *hydraulos* remained more of a curiosity than a concert instrument (Bragard 36). Representations of the instrument have been found on African soil and in France, while parts of a *hydraulos* were excavated at the site of a Roman city near Budapest. During the early Middle Ages, the water organ gradually disappeared from musical life and was replaced by the pneumatic organ. First mentioned in the fourth century AD, this instrument was primarily developed and used in the eastern part of the Roman Empire, and it was to this simpler and more efficient instrument that the future would belong (Geiringer 41).

With the collapse of the Roman Empire and the turmoil caused by the migration of barbaric hordes into Europe, the existence of many of the highly developed instruments of the ancient civilizations became jeopardized. The hostile attitude of the early Christians toward instrumental music added to their neglect. For a long time, instruments were considered by the adherents of the new creed to be relics of pagan worship. This twofold attack on musical instruments produced a kind of vacuum in the middle of the first millennium, which slowly filled during the following centuries through the advent of new-comers from distant lands. From various groups such as merchants, wandering tribes or returning crusaders from the Holy Land, the instruments of the highly civilized Orient found their way to Europe (Geiringer 45-46).

The Moors, who occupied Spain in the eighth century, introduced Arab culture to Europe. From Spain, their instruments spread through France and the rest of Europe largely through the activities of the jongleurs, who were constantly on the move, taking with them their musical instruments. Geiringer writes that with the social rise of the jongleurs the instruments gained full acceptance and were used by laymen and clerics alike. Around the year 900, the monk Tutilo of St. Gallen, Switzerland, is reported to have excelled in his performance of stringed instruments and pipes. Literary sources of the time often referred to them; miniatures in illuminated manuscripts portrayed them; over the portals of Romanesque cathedrals, the statues of crowned elders with instruments in their hands welcomed the congregation. Clearly, musical instruments had been accepted by Western culture (Geiringer 46).

The change and development of musical instruments naturally reflected the evolution of music itself. The ancient modes were giving way to polyphony, a style that began to develop in the ninth century and reached its height in Renaissance vocal music. Polyphonic music shares musical interest equally between parts, which move independently to produce an interwoven texture (Rowley 22).

The direct heritage from Greece and Rome seems to have been rather insignificant, and the lyre is one of the few instruments that might possibly be considered to have passed from antiquity. In the Early Middle Ages, the lyre morphed into an instrument referred to as the *cithara teutonica* and became one of the earliest instruments depicted in medieval manuscripts (Fig. 1.23) (Geiringer 46). Then, after the year 1000, the lyre was gradually pushed into the background by the appearance of other, more efficient plucked instruments. The lyre became played with a bow, and a fingerboard was added running from the soundbox to the yoke. This new instrument, the *crwth* (pronounced "crooth"), became an instrument favored by Welsh bards (Fig. 1.24). The instrument persisted in Celtic Wales, even far into modern times (Geiringer 47). After

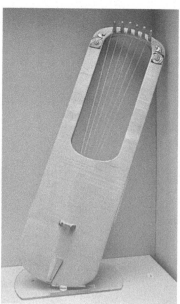

1.23. Medieval lyre player (possibly David?)

1.24. Reconstruction of Sutton Hoo lyre (*cithara teutonica*), seventh century AD

the *crwth* became a bowed lyre, it came to be considered one of the ancestors of the viol (Bragard 43).

In tracing the historical development of musical instruments, one seems to sense the hand of Darwinian natural selection. While the medieval harp harkened back to the *trigonon*, its appearance in Europe can be traced back to Syria (Geiringer 47). During this period of transition, it is unclear in many literary references what type of stringed instrument is being referenced. The following example comes from a poem written by Venantius Fortunatus, who was Bishop of Poitiers from 597 to 600:

> *Romanusque lyre plaudat tibi, barbarus harpa*
> *Graecus achiliaca, chrotta britannia canat.*

> The Romans praise thee with the lyre, the barbarians with the harp,
> The Greek with the Achillean lyre, the Britons with the *crotta*.

As Bragard says of these two lines, four peoples or groups of peoples are named, and each is assigned to an instrument bearing a different name (Bragard 43). It is unclear if the poem is referring to four separate instruments or four names for a single instrument, namely the lyre. Current thinking among scholars is that there are four separate instruments, and the text refers to the barbarians (foreigners) having a harp while the Britons play a *crwth*.

The harp must have been brought to England very early in its Western career. The word "hearpe" appears in the English epic poem *Beowulf* in the eighth century,

1.25. Earliest known picture of a triangular harp in Britain, seventh century AD, *The Story of the Irish Harp*, Richard Hayward, 1974

1.26. Gothic harp, postcard, Germanisches National Museum, Nuremburg

Geiringer writes that the harp may be traced back to tenth-century England, and in a German manuscript of the twelfth or thirteenth century, one finds the harp is called *cythara angelica* (Fig. 1.25).

Ireland, however, was regarded as the true home of the instrument. In the fourteenth century we find an indication of this in Dante, and as late as the seventeenth century the great German musicologist and instrumental expert, Michael Pretorius, speaks of the Irish harp (Geiringer 48). Joan Rimmer writes in her classic work, *The Irish Harp*, that there is a possibility of a link between the Celtic Christian communities of the British Isles and the Christian Near East, Syria, and Egypt. The vertical harps of the Near East were well suited to their dry climate. The harp had a soundbox of thin wood covered with a skin belly. Gut strings twisted round a thin arm made the harp light and easy to carry, even with the box upward. If the same instrument were transported to a cold, damp climate it would become much less stable and efficient. A similar instrument made more robustly, with a soundbox completely of wood, would have a different physical balance. It also had strings fastened to a pin, which passes through a solid frame or neck and is tuned by turning the pin. This means it would have needed a solid string-carrier. Also, it would have been extremely difficult to hold, let alone play, in the Near Eastern box-upwards position. Celtic harps might have originated as insular transformations of a Near Eastern instrument, incorporating certain structural features of robust native lyres and the whole adapted to the climate of northwestern Europe (Rimmer 23-24).

From this point in the early Middle Ages, the development of the harp in Europe diverges into two separate schools and traditions. First was the *cythara anglica*, the small harp of the European age of chivalry (AD 1100-1500), which evolved on the continent first into the elongated "Gothic harp" (Fig. 1.26) and later the double-strung harp, or *arpa doppia*, and thence to the large eighteenth-century salon instruments, the forerunner to the modern concert pedal harp.

1.27. "Brian Boru" harp; this fifteenth/sixteenth-century harp is the oldest surviving Irish harp and erroneously associated with Brian Boru, high king of Ireland (died 1014). Made of willow, 29 strings. Postcard, Trinity College Library, Dublin

1.28. Back view of the Castle Otway harp showing hollowed-out sound-box and soundboard as one unit. Robert Bruce Armstrong, *The Irish and Highland Harps*, 1904

The second was the Irish harp, which developed to a high tradition from the fourteenth through eighteenth centuries in support of the bardic tradition. After the dissolution of the clan system in Ireland in the eighteenth century, the Irish harp passed from popularity and the last remaining harpers gathered in Belfast in 1792, where their compositions were recorded by Edward Bunting.

For our discussion, we will consider the Irish harp first. The harp that is the emblem of Ireland and is depicted on her coinage is a real one (Fig. 1.27), now preserved in Trinity College, Dublin, writes Joan Rimmer. This was the characteristic instrument of Ireland for at least six centuries (Rimmer 1). The major constructional device that sets the "true" Irish harp apart from other European harps, writes Roslyn Rensch, is the hollowing out of the soundbox from a solid piece of timber, with a separate panel forming the back (Fig. 1.28). This solid construction enabled the instrument to withstand the tension of the metal strings (silver, steel, or brass wire), which were apparently rather thick (Rensch 116). The sturdy triangular frame consisted of three distinct parts, which were morticed into each other (since there was no such thing as wood glue in the Middle Ages), and the resulting string tension held the frame in place (Armstrong 34). Only two other objects are always made of willow—the cricket bat and the old-fashioned one-piece clothes peg. Both are dependent for efficiency on the physical properties of willow, on its usual combination of strength and resilience, and these must have been the qualities that made it perfect for the soundboxes of the great Irish harps. The supernatural nature of willow will be covered in more detail in Chapter IV. The forepillar or bow was thick; it curved outward. The neck was deep and heavy with metal tuning pins set low in the neck. The strings were of thick brass; they were plucked with long fingernails, not with the flesh of the fingertips (Rimmer 2). The sweet, resonant, bell-like tone of these strings was a characteristic mentioned enthusiastically by writers that were familiar with the instrument (Rensch 116). The instrument

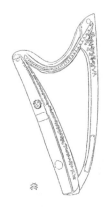

1.29. O'Neill harp, owned by Arthur O'Neill, one of the last Irish harpers, eighteenth century, Armstrong, *The Irish and Highland Harps*, 1904

developed from the low-headed lap instrument of the Middle Ages into the large low-headed version played in the sixteenth and seventeenth centuries and to its final form in the eighteenth century, the high-headed Irish harp (Fig. 1.29) (Rimmer 2).

Originally these instruments were played by men who usually accompanied the poet or bard in his recitation (Fig. 1.30). Perhaps no other musical instrument has been so linked to politics as the Irish harp. Joan Rimmer writes that to the English government officials of sixteenth-century Ireland, harpers, rhymers, Irish chroniclers, bards, and so on were seditious and dangerous persons. Their poetry and music, however, were agreeable even to "gentlemen in the English Pale" and their presence there under any pretext whatever was ultimately forbidden (Rimmer 39). Rimmer also cites William Good, an English Jesuit who taught in Ireland in the middle of the sixteenth century who wrote: "The Irish love music mightily and of all instruments are particularly taken with the harp, which being strung with brass wire and beaten with crooked nails, is very melodious" (Rimmer 39).

Thomas Smith, an English agent, gave this pompously disapproving account of the chanting of a praise poem to a chieftain:

1.30. *Bard and Harper Performing before the Chief of the MacSweynes*, 1581, woodcut, Armstrong, *The Irish and Highland Harps*, 1904

Now comes the rimer that made the rime, with his rakry. The rakry is he that shall utter the rime and the rimer himself sits by with the captain very proudly. He brings with him also his harper who plays all the while that the raky sings the rime . . . and this with more, they look you to have, for destruction of the commonwealth and to the blasphemy of God; and this is the best thing that the rimers cause them to do. (Rimmer 40-41)

Author Charles Acton writes that it is quite certain that Irish harping was highly regarded abroad. Giraldus Cambrensis, who was a cleric at the courts of France and England and a sophisticated European who much disliked the Irish, wrote in 1185:

I find among these people commendable diligence only on musical instruments, on which they are incomparably more skilled than any nation I have seen. Their style is not, as on British instruments to which we are accustomed, deliberate and solemn but quick and lively; nevertheless, the sound is smooth and pleasant. It is remarkable that, with such rapid finger work, the musical rhythm is maintained and that, by unfailingly disciplined art, the integrity of the tune is fully preserved throughout the ornate rhythms and profuse intricate polyphony. (Acton 4)

In the twelfth century, John of Salisbury, describing one of the Crusades in the previous century, wrote that there would have been no music at all if it had not been for the Irish harp as some players must have traveled the great pilgrim routes (Rimmer 41). The skill of the Irish harpers was certainly famous in Europe in the latter part of the sixteenth century when Vincenzo Galilei (father of the astronomer) wrote in 1581:

Among the stringed instruments now played in Italy there is first of all the harp, which is none other than the ancient *cithara* with many strings. The form is indeed different in each case, but only because of the different workmanship of those days, and from the greater number of strings and their thickness. It contains from the lowest note to the highest note more than three octaves.

This most ancient instrument was brought to us (as Dante commented) from Ireland. The people of that island play it a great deal and have done so for many centuries, also it is the special emblem of the realm, where it is depicted and sculptured on public buildings and on coins. From which, it may be deduced to be descended from the Prophet, King David. (Rimmer 41-42)

That the Irish harp had emerged from the Middle Ages as the instrument most identified with Ireland is further evident in its adoption in the royal arms. Richard Hayward writes that the harp as a heraldic device first appeared on the

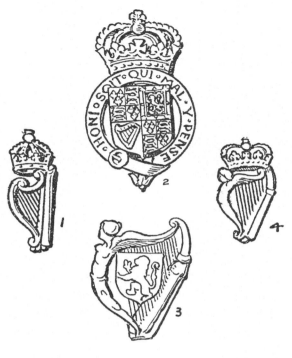

1.31. The harp in the coat of arms of Ireland. The harp as a heraldic device first appeared on the Irish coins of Henry VIII, and not before. Later adopted by Elizabeth I, James I, and Charles I. Richard Hayward, *The Story of the Irish Harp*, 1974

Irish coins of Henry VIII and not before. When Henry became king of Ireland (not lord of Ireland, as was the title before his time), he changed the arms of Ireland from three crowns to three harps, because it is said the three crowns looked like the papal tiara—the triple crown (13)! The harp then passed to the great seal of Elizabeth and with James I it became one of the quarters of the royal shield, a position it maintains to this day. At the time of Charles I, the device assumed the angelic female form, a quality we will see later reflected in cinematic images (Fig. 1.31). In Gaelic society harpers enjoyed a prestige next only to judges, writes Charles Acton (Acton 4). Richard Hayward writes that if one studies the ancient laws of Ireland, it is seen that poets and harpers, compared to bards, were as surgeons are to bone-setters today (Hayward 12). A harper who hoped for any degree of success had to start his tuition before he was ten years of age with great attention and practice required of him so that by the time he was eighteen, he was expected to be fully qualified as a professional. He had to become the absolute master of the three required styles of music: the *suantrai*, which no one could hear without falling into a delightful sleep; the *goltrai*, which no one could hear without bursting into tears or lamentations; and the *geantrai*, which no one could hear without bursting into long and loud laughter (Hayward 5).

The harp was certainly played as an accompaniment to the singing or recitation of historical and political poems and the genealogical praises of the kings

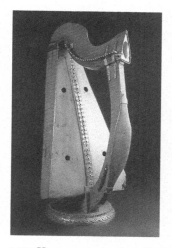

1.32. Harp or clarsach, called the Lamont harp, West Highlands, about 1500, postcard, Museum of Scotland

1.33. Court harper, illustration from *Music throughout the World*, Marian Cotton and Adelaide Bradburn, 1953, Summy-Birchard, Evanston, IL

and chiefs. As such, it was proscribed by the English; and yet they continued its use as the national emblem of Ireland, which it still is; and Ireland is the only country in the world with a musical instrument as its national emblem (Acton 4). As to this heraldic use of the harp, Henry Howard, Earl of Northampton and Earl Marshal of England, was reputed to have remarked in 1603: "The best reason I can observe for the bearing (of the Irish harp in the English royal arms) is it resembles that country in being such an instrument that it requires more cost to keep in tune than it is worth" (Heyward 13).

In medieval times, writes Joan Rimmer, the harp had generally been an aristocratic, high-art instrument (Fig. 1.32), and nowhere more so than in Ireland. A harper was a skilled specialist, and no poor man could have maintained or hired one, any more than he could maintain a racehorse today (Fig. 1.33). The patrons of men of learning, of poets, reciters, and harpers, were the Gaelic Irish aristocracy, the Norman-Irish who eventually became indistinguishable in English government eyes from the native lords and later, the powerful Anglo-Irish families (Rimmer 37). One reason that the harper may have held a high position in the household might have been the long fingernails required to play the brass strings. These were often a liability; for political recrimination, many a harper had his fingernails cut off by the English. As a general rule, Irish harps were strung with metal, usually brass, but in later years, some larger harps were strung with gut. Author Richard Hayward mentions a harp from about 1657 that bore the following Gaelic inscription on its forepillar: "May you never want a string while there's guts in an Englishman" (Heyward 15). The political nature

1.34. *Erin*, carved by Pearce and Sharp in 1889 for the National Bank in College Green, Dublin. She is surrounded by Irish symbols—the hound and the harp. Jean Sheehy and George Mott, *The Rediscovery of Ireland's Past, The Celtic Revival 1830-1930*, Thames and Hudson, 1980

of the harp continued well into the nineteenth century and the harp together with the shamrock, the Irish wolfhound, and the round tower, became the national emblems of Ireland. During the Celtic Revival from 1830 to 1930, these images appear in Irish art, sculpture, and architecture (Fig. 1.34) (Sheehy 9).

During this period, the form of the harp assumed the feminine angelic style, which was first introduced on the arms of Charles I. Like the ancient Greeks, the Irish attributed the invention of the harp to Celtic mythology. In 1845, the artist Daniel Maclise provided the famous illustration *The Origin of the Harp* to accompany the poem of the same name in Thomas Moore's *Irish Melodies* (Fig. 1.35). Jeanne Sheehy writes that Moore provided an abundance of Irish sentiment, cast in a romantic mold, but toned down, and made respectable or converted the wild harp of Erin into a musical snuffbox (Sheehy 46). Moore got the subject from Edward Hudson, whom he had visited in Kilmainham Gaol after his involvement in the rebellion of 1798. To pass the time, Hudson had made a large drawing on the wall of his cell representing a lovesick mermaid who was weeping for her true love when her long hair spilled over her arm, forming the strings of a harp (Sheehy 49). A stanza in Moore's "The Origin of the Harp" describes it beautifully:

> Still her bosom rose fair—still her cheeks smil'd the same—
> While her sea-beauties gracefully form'd the light frame;
> And her hair, as, let loose, o'er her white arm it fell,
> Was changed to bright chords, uttering melody's spell.

The Origin of the Harp

'Tis believ'd that this Harp, which I wake now
for thee,
Was a Siren of old, who sung under the sea;
And who often, at eve, thro' the bright waters rov'd.
To meet, on the green shore, a youth whom she lov'd.

But she lov'd him in vain, for he left her to weep,
And in tears, all the night her gold tresses to steep;
Till heav'n look'd with pity on true-love so warm,
And chang'd to this soft Harp the sea-maiden's form.

1.35. *The Origin of the Harp* illustration by Daniel Maclise for Thomas Moore's *Irish Melodies*, 1845. Jeanne Sheehy and George Mott, *The Rediscovery of Ireland's Past, The Celtic Revival 1830–1930*, Thames and Hudson, 1980

The romantic feminization of the Irish harp occurred at about the same time the European harp was developing into the salon instrument of the nineteenth century. We will see how these images turn up in films.

While the Irish harp with its metal strings, bell-like tone, robust construction, and seditious political reputation dominated the British Isles, its cousin, the *cythara angelica*, underwent its own development on the continent, evolving its own mythology to become "the heavenly instrument" of Christian iconography and ultimately resulting in what we recognize as the modern pedal harp. It was stated earlier in this chapter that from the very outset Christianity was in favor of vocal music and strongly opposed instrumental music. Alexander Buchner writes that for many centuries the organ was considered an instrument of luxury, coming from the court of the emperors of the eastern part of the Roman Empire, and it was even asserted that the Devil's voice sounded from the organ's pipes. The few remaining classical instruments were played only by minstrels and itinerant entertainers. On the other hand, the instruments

1.36. Ancient hydraulis mosaic at the Roman villa at Nenning. An organist and horn player entertain at a gladiator match, Museum fur Vor und Fruhgeschichte, Saarbrücken, Germany, screenshot

mentioned in the Old Testament—particularly the harp of David—enjoyed great reverence though they had never been seen by anyone. An illustration in an illuminated English manuscript of the twelfth century contrasts the instruments condoned by the Church with those that were denounced, even contrasting God's musicians with the Devil's music-makers. Among the approved instruments were the monochord, chimes, pan pipes, organ, harp, and cornett, while the rebec, horn, and drums were the Devil's instruments (Buchner 16).

Buchner comments, "With the end of ovations to Roman emperors at the Capitol and celebrations in honor of pagan deities in temples, the musical instruments that had played such an important role on these occasions of pomp and glory were also silenced and forgotten. Most of the musical instruments of the Greeks and Romans disappeared and fell into oblivion" (Buchner 19). Amazingly, considering earlier condemnations, the organ (*hydraulos*) (Fig. 1.36) and the harp (*trigonon*) were two classical instruments to be adopted by the Church and carried forward into the future.

In the sixth century, Bishop Isidore of Seville left us an interesting work on celestial music, the illustrations for which became a very popular subject for many medieval artists. It is only natural that the celestial orchestra included all musical instruments known at the time, played by angels and the spirits of saints. The *musica coelestis* inspired the imagination of many artists—for example, those who executed the sculptured decoration on church portals, some of which depicted figures playing various musical instruments. This iconographical material confirms the importance of musical instruments in medieval music culture, which owed much to jongleurs and minnesingers (Buchner 16).

Early Christian iconography transformed Orpheus (who was the son of Apollo) into King David. This would have a profound effect on the survival of the harp as both a symbol and as a musical instrument. Orpheus playing his lyre to assembled beasts is a subject frequently encountered in Roman art. The association of the player surrounded by animals was transferred in the early days of Christianity to symbolize the figure of the Good Shepherd and appears in the Christian catacombs. His audience, which at the beginning contains a pair of lions, becomes reduced little by little to a flock of sheep, and Orpheus or the Good Shepherd then is metamorphosed into King David with his "harp" (Marcuse 366). Thus, the images of the triangular harp appear in the ninth-century Utrecht Psalter, and a straight column harp is depicted as being played by King David in the twelfth-century Codex 1879 of the Vienna National Library (Marcuse 388). Like Orpheus who could charm the animals, David was remembered as being able to soothe King Saul with the strings of his harp, and he becomes identified with the instrument in Christian iconography while the mantle of the "Good Shepherd" is passed into New Testament references. Karl Geiringer writes of the *cythara anglica*:

> The European harp of the Middle Ages consisted of three parts (in contrast to Asiatic harps which were built in two parts). At the back is the soundbox to which metal strings are attached. Above is the neck, set at a sharp angle, often curved a little inwards, and furnished with tuning-pins, turned by a tuning key. In front, supporting the neck, is the pillar, sometimes with a slight outward curve. The shape of the whole is heavy and squat, rather like an equilateral triangle.
>
> Clearly, this new instrument, distributed rapidly throughout the west, would have at once come into competition with the lyre, since their uses were so similar. The outcome of this rivalry left no room for doubt. The lyre possessed strings of equal length only; if they were too thin or too tightly strung they were liable to break. The lyre, therefore, had only a small, middle compass. The strings of the harp, on the other hand, were of different lengths, so that the difficulty of a limited compass did not arise. Thus music calling for an ever-increasing compass naturally had to turn from the lyre to the harp. (Geiringer 48)

Although medieval harps, like Irish harps, sometimes had metal strings, most instruments were strung with sheep gut, which resulted in a softer tone. The almost inaudible tone of these light harps was amplified using bray pins—small pegs that were inserted into the string shoes in the soundbox and resonated or buzzed as the strings were plucked. This gave the harp a kazoo-like effect enabling it to be heard when playing with other instruments. In his *De Proprietatibus Rerum* (c. 1250), the thirteenth-century Franciscan Bartholomaeus Anglicus warned against mixing the gut of sheep and wolves:

1.37. "Angel with A Harp," detail from the painting *The Betrothal of St. Catherine* by Hans Memling, Flemish, about 1465-1494, Christmas card, Metropolitan Museum of Art

1.38. Detail from Hieronymus Bosch's *Garden of Earthly Delights,* fifteenth century

1.39. West Highland harp from Lude, Perthshire: said to have been given by Queen Mary to Beatrix Gardyne of Banchory about 1500 AD, postcard, National Museum of Scotland

> strengis imade of guttes of wolves destroye and freti and corrumpid
> strengis imade of guttis of schiepe if hit so be pat be so isette among them
> as in fethle or in harpe. (Remnant 20)

The later medieval development of the European harp form had two main stages. The first was the Romanesque harp; the second was the gothic harp. The stout Romanesque harp was the continuation of the *cythara angelica*, which had a curving pillar, and the distinction between three parts—body, neck, and pillar—was emphasized by ornamentation. The slender gothic harp had an almost straight pillar, and the construction tended to unify rather than to separate the three parts, so they seemed to be made of one piece of wood. This transition from the first type of harp to the second type took place about 1430 (Sachs 264). This is the familiar instrument held by numerous angels in High Renaissance paintings (Fig. 1.37), woodcuts by Albrecht Durer, works of Hieronymus Bosch (Fig. 1.38), and various portraits of King David. Of all indoor instruments, the harp had the highest rank; members of royal families and aristocracy played it. When it was played skillfully, it would "destroy the fends myght;" the evil spirits fled, the rivers stopped flowing, and the cattle forgot to eat (Figs. 1.39-1.41) (Sachs 264).

1.40. Daniel Maclise, *Alfred the Saxon King Disguised as a Minstrel in the Tent of Guthrun the Dane*, 1852. His harp is based on the original Brian Boru.

1.41. Detail from Daniel Maclise, *The Marriage of Strongbow and Eva*, 1854 (National Gallery of Ireland). The figure of the bard, symbol for Maclise of the Celts' departed glory, holds a harp similar to the Brian Boru. *The Rediscovery of Ireland's Past: The Celtic Revival 1830-1930*, Thames and Hudson, 1980

Except for an increase in size and the number of strings, the form of the harp remained practically unchanged from the late Middle Ages until the eighteenth century (Marcuse 390). Around the 1700s, however, the harp entered a period of crisis. Throughout its development, the harp has been tuned diatonically, that is, there were no accidentals like the black keys on the piano. This became a liability as the instrument had to be retuned between compositions and could not cope adequately with the increasing chromaticism in music. For a time, therefore, the harp gave way in importance to the fretted lute on which all semitones could easily be played. To retain its place as a viable musical instrument, the harp therefore would have to become chromatic (Remnant 21).

The search for a chromatic harp would result in the development of the double and triple harps with additional rows of strings and an increase in size. Marcuse writes that harps appear to have been among the most versatile of seventeenth-century instruments, participating with equal ease in drawing-room or tavern music (Marcuse 392). The triple harp originated in Italy in the late sixteenth century and died out on the Continent a century later; at the same time, it appeared in Wales, where it became the national instrument (Marcuse 393).

The harp, according to Sachs, may owe its advancement at the end of the eighteenth century to the victory of the piano over the harpsichord. As long as the harpsichord existed, between the fifteenth and eighteenth centuries, the harp, which was also a plucked instrument, was regarded as inferior in chords, polyphony, and technique. With the disappearance of the harpsichord, the field was clear for an instrument like the harp, provided it could be given a chromatic scale (Sachs 398). The inconvenience of multiple rows of strings too closely spaced for ease in plucking was obviated in the late seventeenth century by the invention of the hook harp, which allowed a string to be shortened a semitone by twisting a small hook against the string. This cumbersome but workable solution soon evolved into a pedal mechanism whereby the string could be shortened or lengthened by depressing a foot pedal, which connected through the harp's forepillar to the harmonic curve. The invention is credited to two Bavarians, Hochrucker and Vetter of Nuremberg.

Sebastian Erard of Paris patented the pedal harp in 1762 and later developed the double-pedal harp in London in 1810, having left France during the revolution. Erard had made the harp fully chromatic with a twelve-note scale. This became the standard for the modern pedal harp, which has been in use ever since. He also made the strings tighter and thicker, strengthened the sound chest, and decorated the head and base of the pillar with Greek maidens and lyre players, causing the instrument to be called the "Grecian harp" (Fig. 1.42). In 1836, his nephew Pierre Erard produced his own "Gothic harp," identified by its angels and Gothic arches (Marcuse 395).

"The improvements made by Sebastian Erard greatly changed the position of the harp in society," writes Marcuse. "The single action instruments had been played not only by professionals, but also by numerous amateurs including Queen Marie Antoinette of France, and many harps from this period remain to decorate the stately homes of Europe.

"The new instrument, being larger, heavier and more complicated to play

1.42. Single-action pedal harp. From Bochsa's *Standard Tutor for the Harp,* Ashdown, London. Rensch, *Harps & Harpists,* Bloomington, Indiana University Press, 1989

was too difficult for many harpists who, recognizing its superior qualities, gave up the harp altogether for the piano" (Marcuse 396).

"All of this improvement in the harp took place when the instrument had become a salon fixture fashionably suitable for ladies of leisure. Developing at a time when the piano was striving for an ever increasing power, the harp was particularly assigned to the feminine province of musical expression, where its ornamental shape was an added attraction," writes Sachs. "It has been a lady's instrument since the days of Marie Antoinette, both at home and in the orchestra, and composers have stressed its aptitude for tenderness and mystery. Thus, the harp expressed one of the most typical moods of romantic feeling" (Sachs 401).

Irish harping continued in its traditional manner until the end of the eighteenth century and the final breakup of the clan system and the dissolution of the old Irish society. For all practical purposes, the Irish harp tradition was dead, and no one continued playing the wire-strung harp. What remained of the harp tradition in Ireland moved to the pedal harp when it arrived from Europe in 1820. Henceforth, in Europe the future belonged to this most recent version of the ancient instrument.

HERMES THE TRICKSTER

Zeus, the giver of counsel, rejoiced to have made them such comrades, and down to this day Apollo, son of Leto, and Hermes are friendly, as is shown by the gift of the lyre that Hermes gave the far-darter, which Apollo so skillfully strums, embracing it in his arms.

—Homeric Hymn to Hermes (1–512)

And to be instructed in music is precisely to know how all this system of things is ordered, and what divine plan has distributed it. For this order, having brought all individual things into unity by creative reason, will produce as it were a most sweet and true harmony, and a divine melody.

—Asclepius II.13

In the pseudo-*Homeric Hymn to Hermes*, written around the sixth century BC, the infant god Hermes invented the lyre from the shell of a tortoise. According to the story, the babe Hermes was the boisterous son of the nymph Maya and Zeus, the father of the gods. As a babe, Hermes leaps instantly out of his crib and dashes into the outside world where he comes upon a turtle, which he kills and takes the shell from to construct a lyre, becoming "the first to manufacture songs" (Davis 20). He then proceeds to steal the cattle herd belonging to his brother Apollo, hiding them in a cave. When Apollo discovers the theft and confronts Hermes, the young god denies any knowledge of the act, claiming his infancy would have prevented him from doing what Apollo charges. Hermes fools him by proclaiming oaths that, like the slickest of legal contracts, writes Erik Davis, do not mean what they seem to say (Davis 20). The two travel to Olympus to resolve the conflict. Hermes plays the lyre and Apollo is so taken by the sweetness of the lyre that he tells Hermes: "What you have there is worth fifty cattle, I know about music; I accompany the Muses when they dance to the sound of flutes; but I have never heard music such as this, music full

2.1. Hermes/Mercury,
nineteenth-century
illustration

of invitations to gaiety and love and sleep." Hermes replied with characteristic
shrewdness, "I am not selfish; it would be a pleasure to teach you the secret of
my instrument, just as Zeus taught you the art of prophecy. It is indeed a marvelous instrument in the hands of a true artist. In return you must be generous
and share your patronage over cattle with me." And so a bargain was struck—
Hermes received the neat herd's staff from Apollo, and Apollo received the lyre
from Hermes. The two brothers drove the cattle back to the meadow at the foot
of Mount Olympus, lessening the tedium of the journey with music on the lyre
(Brown 70).

Then Apollo said to Hermes, "I am afraid you will steal my lyre and bow, for
Zeus has put you in charge of establishing the art of exchange on Earth. I won't
feel secure until you take a solemn oath." So Hermes swore he would not steal
Apollo's property and in return Apollo swore he would consider no friend dearer
than Hermes; he also promised to give him a magic wand empowered to execute
all the good decrees pronounced by Apollo in his capacity as the oracular inter-
preter of the will of Zeus. In addition, Apollo put Hermes in charge of the whole
animal kingdom, wild and domestic, and Hermes alone would be messenger to
Hades (Fig. 2.1) (Brown 70).

"The Greeks make no bones about the fact that Hermes is a thief," writes
Erik Davis. But Hermes's banditry should not be confused with appropriations
based on raw power. The information trickster works through cleverness and
stealth; he is not the mugger or the thug, but the hacker, the spy, the master-
mind. When Hermes makes off with Apollo's cattle, he sports specially designed
footwear that leaves no tracks, and he forces the animals to walk backward in
order to trick his pursuers. The conflict between the aristocratic lord Apollo
and the young upstart god Hermes is instructive. Apollo can be considered the

god of science in its ideal form: pure, ordering, embodying the solar world of clarity and light (Davis 20-21).

In his book, *Hermes the Thief: The Evolution of a Myth*, Norman Brown delineates one of Hermes's cultural implications, the trickster. First, the term "trickster" or "thief" implies guile and stealth. "Skill at the oath" means guile or cunning in the use of the oath and derives from the primitive idea that an oath was binding only in its literal sense; a cunning person might legitimately manipulate it in order to deceive. Hermes is also the patron of another special kind of trickery—the trickery involved in sexual seduction as in Hesiod's myth of Pandora, the Greek version of Eve, "the source of all woe" (Brown 8).

A review of the mythology of Hermes the Trickster shows that his trickery is never represented as a rational device, but rather as a manifestation of magical power. Thus, Hermes uses magic to commit successful theft. Other types of magical power are attributed to Hermes in the oldest myths in which he is the trickster rather than the thief.

The imprisonment and release of demons are magical exercises. Both Hermes's magical power to release and attendant power to bind are illustrated in the so-called cursing tablets, which are inscribed with curses against persons named on them and then buried in the ground. The Greek word for these cursing tablets means "bindings," and a number of them invoke Hermes as "the one who holds down" or as "the spell binder." Because of his power to bind and release, Hermes was the god who prevented the souls of the dead from leaving the tomb. Related to this same power of binding is the "skill at the oath," which Hermes bestowed upon Autolycus. An oath is a curse, a magic formula that binds parties to a given action. Hermes is the master of the magic formulae that bind (Brown 12-13).

In the myth of Pandora, Hermes's gift of "lies and deceitful words and stealthy disposition" is the gift of guile in sexual seduction. Seduction was, throughout the Greek world, a magic art, employing love charms and compulsive magic directed at the person desired, and supplicatory rituals invoking the deities of love—of whom Hermes was one, and Aphrodite the foremost. A lover might invoke Aphrodite, "weaver of tricks," or Hermes the Trickster. In fact, Hermes and Aphrodite were frequently associated in ritual, and even combined in the figure Hermaphroditus. One epithet, "the whisperer," which was shared by Hermes, Aphrodite, and Eros, underlies the connection between Hermes the master of love magic and Hermes the master of magic words (Brown 14).

Hermes is not only the master of magic words, writes Brown, he also has a magic wand, the caduceus. Thus, Hermes was a magician and a trickster. Both these attributes shed light on the primitive concept of magic. Its original meaning was "secret action." To the primitive mind "secret action" means magic—the kind worked in the powers of seduction and the magic formulae of oaths (Brown 18). With this somewhat fuller understanding of Hermes the Thief, Brown writes, it

2.2. *Apollo and the Crow*, white-ground kylix, 400 BC, Archeological Museum, Delphi, Greece

is possible to connect with several of the god's other mythological roles, which seem unrelated—Hermes the Craftsman, the god of boundaries, crossroads, and merchants and the marketplace, as well as of the lyre.

Hermes's invention of the lyre and also the panpipes makes him the archetypal craftsman who cleverly constructs things, and this inventiveness breaks the boundaries of the tribal habits and social customs. Thus, Hermes becomes a boundary-crosser, both physically and psychologically. The boundary-crosser is the hallmark of the shaman who travels between worlds. Brown writes that the magico-religious ideas surrounding trade on the boundary in the age of village communities persisted, in modified form, after the village community had been absorbed into the city-state.

Hermes followed trade from the perimeter of the village community to the center of the city-state, the agora, and became Hermes *agoraios*. The mythology of Hermes was affected not only by the transference of the market from the boundary to the city agora, but also by the concentration of commercial activity in the hands of a specialized profession of merchants—or "professional boundary-crossers," as they are called in Homer. The merchant, the pioneer, the craftsman, the unskilled laborer, together these form the Third Estate of Greek social history, with whose fortunes Hermes's destiny was closely bound (Brown 43-45). Brown goes on to state that the underlying theme of the *Hymn to Hermes* was political in that it attempted to put the competing cults of Hermes and Apollo on an equal footing and thus reinforce the democratic basis of Greek society. Hermes (the commoner) had become bound to Apollo (the aristocrat). Both the lyre and the *kithara* became the instruments of Apollo: music would become the art of the aristocracy (Fig. 2.2). Hermes the Trickster helps us understand the powerful archetypal connection between magic, tricks, and technology. But he is merely a shadow of his former self, which originally came to Greece from across the Mediterranean in Egypt.

According to Melville Clark, the story of the invention of the harp is older than the Greek tradition:

> Be it fact or legend, history has given to the Egyptian priest, Hermes, the credit for the invention of the lyre, which is known as the ancestor of the harp. In the calm of a balmy summer evening, Hermes, an Egyptian priest, was strolling along the banks of the River Nile deeply engrossed in thought, when suddenly a strange and intensely beautiful sound arrested his attention. Delighted, he looked about for the source. He was alone—all nature was at rest—still that weird, illusive sound vibrated in the air. At his feet lay a beautiful shell. Impatiently his foot brushed it from the path, when once again that musical sound burst forth. Stooping he lifted the shell and upon examining it closely, found that its former inhabitant had departed and its sinews, dried by the sun, were stretched across the shell, which when accidentally touched by his foot, had produced the strange and most remarkable sound.
>
> This man, Hermes, High Priest of Osiris, was founder of the Egyptian law and religious ceremonies; he taught the Egyptians the science of hieroglyphics, the culture of the olive, the measurement of land, and by this little incident enacted on the river banks, evolved the musical instrument which developed into the harp. (Clark 4)

This fanciful story is an apt introduction to the Egyptian god Thoth from whom the Greek Hermes was descended. Thoth, who was venerated in Egypt from at least 3000 BC, is said to be the inventor of sacred hieroglyphic writing. His figure can be seen in many temples and tombs (Fig. 2.3) (Freke 7). He is the dispatcher of divine messages and recorder of all human deeds. In the Great Hall of Judgment, the afterlife court of the god Osiris, it was Thoth who established whether the deceased had acquired spiritual knowledge and purity, and so deserved a place in the heavens (Fig. 2.4). Thoth was said to have revealed to the Egyptians all knowledge on astronomy, architecture, geometry, medicine, and religion. The Greeks, always in awe of the knowledge and spirituality of the Egyptians, identified Thoth with their own god Hermes, the messenger of the gods and guider of souls into the realm of the dead. To distinguish the Egyptian Hermes from their own, the Greeks sometime later gave him the title "Trismegistus," meaning "Thrice-Great," to honor his sublime wisdom. The books attributed to him became collectively known as the *Hermetica* (Freke 7).

Patrick Boylan writes that Thoth was in many ways as ancient and as independent a god as Osiris himself. As secretary or scribe of Osiris, Thoth is therefore the companion to the chief god of Egypt when the latter goes on his administrative journeys (Boylan 58). Thoth, as trustworthy minister and scribe of Ra, kept for him the great book of government (the "divine book") in which every detail of Ra's empire and its administration would be carefully noted.

2.3. Egyptian god Thoth (Tehuty)

2.4. The god Anubis weighs the heart of the deceased and Thoth records the results, from *The Egyptian Book of the Dead*, Chronicle Books, San Francisco

The idea for the divine book seems to have been borrowed from the methods of government administration in Egypt. Just as the pharaoh received reports from his ministers and just as the details of all administrative work in Egypt were carefully recorded, so must the king of the world, the sun god Ra, have official reports and official records (Boylan 60).

It may be that Thoth's confidential position as minister and chief scribe in the government of Ra is due partly to the native sentiment that the moon is a representative of Ra, a sort of *locum tenens* for the sun god.[1] Thus, the two great astral deities would naturally, between them, rule the world (Boylan 61). The most familiar symbols of Thoth are the ibis and the ape.[2]

Plutarch recognizes that Hermes or Thoth is the source of cosmic order. Hermes cut the sinews of Typhon or Set, and from them made the cords whence are derived, ultimately, chords or the harmonies of world-order. "Establishing the laws like the Lord of Hsrt or Thoth," is a constantly recurring epithet of the Pharaohs in the latter-day Alexandria period. From the time of the New Kingdom Thoth was regarded as the source of law, and therefore, as the founder of the social order. Also, it was usual for Egyptian shrines to boast their complete conformity with the plans and prescriptions of Thoth. The hieroglyphic inscriptions on the temple-walls, which are intended not less for ornament than instruction, are according to the directions of Thoth. He was regarded as the author of ecclesiastical architecture and the laws of sacred geometry. (Boylan 89-91)

Thoth was not only the architect of the temple; as "lord of the divine words," he also devised the rituals carried out in the temples. Hence his lordship over the formulae of ritual and cult. To Thoth was assigned to the duty of superintending the celebration of ritual ceremonial and in Thoth was found the source of all such mysterious power as was contained in charms, spells, and all invocations of the gods (Boylan 95). Thoth's relation to literature and speech, and his role of secretary to the sun god, would, of course, also tend to connect him with Hermes. Plutarch quite obviously views Thoth as Hermes (Boylan 140). As god of wisdom and orderer of the cosmos, Thoth's word has power to call things into being. It is little wonder, then, that he is endowed with great magical powers.

To work, magic presupposes a special gnosis. The magician claims to possess a higher and deeper knowledge than others, a knowledge of the secret nature of things, and of the hidden connections that hold things together. Thoth, as the wisest of the gods, became for the Egyptian, of necessity, the archetypal magician. He was also the skilled physician who healed the damaged eye of Horus and was the patron of physicians. Magic and medicine were at one time merely different names for the same science. Thoth, as physician, was already skilled in magic (Boylan 124). Thoth's role as psychopomp also contributed to his early identification with the Greek Hermes—who is likewise the guide of the dead (Boylan 140).

The origins of the *Hermetica* attributed to Thoth/Hermes are shrouded in mystery. The surviving works attributed to Hermes are not written in ancient Egyptian hieroglyphics, but in Greek, Latin, and Coptic. These writings were assembled in in the city of Alexandria in Egypt during the second and third centuries AD, when Alexandria was the intellectual center of the Hellenistic world, surpassing even Athens. It had become the melting pot of ideas and the Alexandrians were renowned for their thirst for knowledge. The enlightened Greek ruler Ptolemy I founded a library and museum in which human beings first systematically collected the wisdom of the world.

Within Alexandria's hothouse religious atmosphere, the gods were constantly being remixed and retooled, writes Erik Davis. Terra-cotta figures from the time show Egyptian deities cavorting in Greek togas. This eclectic spirit of recombinant religion led to the fusion of the Greek Hermes with the Egyptian god Thoth and from this crossbreed emerged Hermes Trismegistus (Davis 27). Garth Fowden writes that Hermes Trisgemistus, then, was the cosmopolitan, Hellenistic Hermes, Egyptianized through his assimilation to Thoth, and in fact known throughout the Roman world as "the Egyptian" par excellence. To some extent this intermingling of Egyptian and Greek theology and Hellenistic philosophy produced a sum that was greater than its parts, a divinity who deserved his place among the *dei magni* of the pagan pantheon that presided over the Roman world (Fowden 24).

Given this background on Hermes's Egyptian heritage, let us return to Greece for a final look at Hermes the Trickster. Both Hermes and Apollo are associated with the lyre, and both are gods. Yet in Greek mythology there is a third major personality involved with music and the lyre. I refer to the mortal hero Orpheus.

W. K. C. Guthrie writes that the individuality of Orpheus refuses to be submerged. There are times when he seems on the point of becoming merged with the lyre-playing Apollo and others when we wonder whether he is only an incarnation of the Thracian Dionysus. Orpheus is first and foremost the musician with magic in his notes. Aeschylus knew him as the man who charmed all nature with his singing. As Apollo had no serious rival among the gods, though Hermes might have invented the lyre, so Orpheus among the heroes was supreme in the art of music. The power of the lyre was able to soften the hearts of warriors and turn their thoughts to peace, just as it could tame the wildest of beasts (Fig. 2.5). Not only animals but men gathered round to listen to the song. Closely allied with music in the Greek mind was magic, so that the name of Orpheus was naturally associated with charms, spells, and incantations. Orpheus was the prophet or founder of a particular type of mystery religion, which seems

2.5. Orpheus with lyre charms the animals, Roman mosaic

to have been a modification of the mysteries of Dionysus. His teachings were embodied in sacred writings called the Orphic Hymns, which were sung. Such was the belief in his antiquity that, coupled with his reputation as a poet, some claimed he was as the inventor of writing, while others thought of him as so old that they could not believe he wrote down his own poems (Guthrie 39-40).

Orpheus was regarded not as a god but as a hero in the Greek sense of someone who could claim close friendship with the gods, and had certain superhuman powers, but who had to live the ordinary life span and die like any other mortal. The answer to the question "Who was the god of the Orphic religion?" can only be Dionysus. Orpheus was a religious founder, and the religion he founded was a species of the Bacchic cult.

Iamblichus tells us Pythagoras and Plato read through the stelae of Hermes with the help of native priests during their respective visits to Egypt (Fowden 30). This is a clear indication of the perceived influence of Hermes/Thoth on Greek mystery religions such as Orphism, which were introduced in the sixth century. According to Proclus the Platonic Successor, "All theology among the Greeks is sprung from the mystical doctrine of Orpheus," writes David Fideler, and hence it is with the name of this mythical cultural hero that all inquiry into Western spirituality must begin. Everyone has heard the story of how Orpheus attempted to rescue his wife Eurydice from the underworld. His music had not only the power to stay the gates of death, but the celestial harmonies that sprang from his magical lyre charmed all of nature. When he played, the animals and beasts gathered round, unable to resist the power of his song. Herodotus refers to "Orphic and Bacchic" as meaning actually "Egyptian and Pythagorean," and the Orphics in Greece were the first to teach the immortality of the soul, a doctrine of transmigration or reincarnation, the goal of salvation, and the means through which an individual might transcend the cycle of births altogether (Fideler 1993, 202).

Traditional accounts agreed that Orpheus traveled to Egypt, invented the alphabet, taught Greece the mysteries of initiation, and served as a priest of both Dionysus and Apollo. Orpheus taught that "the eternal essence of number is the most providential principle of the universe," and that there is a distinct relation between the nature of the gods and certain "intelligible numbers." The Platonist Syrianus (second century AD) observed that "the Pythagoreans received from the theology of Orpheus the principles of intelligible and intellectual numbers," and the Platonists themselves were actually a continuing link in the golden chain of the Orphic-Pythagorean tradition (Fideler 1993, 202).

It has been said that numbers were not invented; they were discovered as archetypes of orderliness. Nowhere was this more important than in ancient Greece. David Fideler writes: "Everyone agrees that the ancient Greeks possessed an affinity for the principles of harmony and proportion. This is evident in all the artifacts of Greek civilization, ranging from vases to architecture, from household items to temples and statuary. Given this intimate awareness and love of harmony, proportion, and symmetry, it is not surprising that the Greeks perfected the study of these principles in the realms of science and philosophy" (Fideler 1993, 53).

> Pythagoras, the first Greek to call himself a *philosopher*, "a lover of wisdom," taught that all things are arranged and defined by Number. For the Pythagoreans, Number represents a celestial power working in the divine sphere, a veritable blueprint of creation. Consequently, Number is itself divine and associated with the divinities.
>
> Whence Pythagoras derived this notion is uncertain. It could well be that his experiments on the monochord, a one-stringed musical instrument, revealed to him the basic numerical ratios which underlie the structure of harmony and music. It could be that the idea of the divine primacy of Number is a doctrine which Pythagoras received during his sojourns among the Babylonian and Egyptian priests. According to Iamblichus, Pythagoras received the doctrine from his initiation into the mysteries of Orphism. He concludes that Pythagoras "learnt from the Orphic writers that the essence of the gods is defined by Number." (Fideler 1993, 25-26)

For a practical illustration of these Pythagorean ideas and their relation to the archetypal nature of the harp, we need only consider several Greek words and their mathematical relationship to each other and the Pythagorean ideas of harmony.[3]

A curious fact of the Greek and Hebrew alphabets is that the letters also stood for numbers. Before the introduction of Arabic numerals, both the Greeks and the Jews used their alphabets for notation. In Greek, it worked as follows: the first group of letters (alpha-theta) in the alphabet represented units, the next group of letters (iota-pi) represented tens, and the last group of letters (rho-omega) represented hundreds. Thus, alpha = 1, beta = 2, gamma = 3, kappa = 20, sigma = 200, and so on.

A consequence of this alphabetic notation is that words can be represented as numbers and that numbers can be represented as words. Fideler writes in *Jesus Christ, Sun of God*, that the earliest known usage of this practice, known as gematria, is recorded on a Babylonian clay tablet. It states that the ruler Sargon II (720 BC) ordered that the wall of Khorsabad be constructed to have a length of 16,283 cubits, the numerical value of his name (Fideler 1993, 26-27). The word *gematria*, however, is based on the Greek word *geometria*, or "geometry," and as we shall see, there exists definitive evidence that gematria constituted a sacred language of Greek theology and was in use before the time of Plato.

To determine the numerical value of any Greek or Hebrew word by gematria, one simply adds together the standard numerical equivalents of the individual letters to produce a final sum for the value of the entire word. Thus, the Greek word HERMES = 353 (5 + 100 + 40 + 200 = 353). Since the decimal point was unused in ancient mathematics, HERMES, 353, may also be expressed as .353, 3.53, 35.3, or 3530. Unity or the First Cause may be expressed as 1, 10, 100, 1,000.

Fideler writes that Hermes and Apollo, the two Greek gods of music, are "brothers," the sons of Zeus. The relations between the two divinities may be represented mathematically through the harmonic and geometric principles of mediation, which underlie the structure of the musical scale. In the equation below, we take HERMES, 353, and APOLLO, 1061, to represent the extremes to be harmonized. It will then be discovered that the geometric mean between HERMES and APOLLO is 612, Zeus, while the harmonic mean between the two is 531, LYRE (Fideler 1993, 220):

HERMES	LYRE	ZEUS	APOLLO
353	531	612	1061
	$\dfrac{2\,AB}{}$		
A	$\dfrac{2\,AB}{A+B}$	$\sqrt{A \times B}$	B
	Harmonic mean	Geometric mean	

It is not my intention to launch into a mathematical discussion and I offer no more than this very brief explanation of a very deep and fascinating subject. One should consult Fideler's book for an in-depth study of these relationships where it will be shown that the number values of APOLLO, ZEUS, and HERMES precisely relate to one another through the ratio of the square root of three with the exact mathematical values, starting from 1061, the number of Apollo. It is remarkable that the canon of Greek gematria presupposes that the names of the major divinities and mythological figures were consciously codified in relation to the natural ratios of geometry to equal specific numerical values. This notion may initially strike the modern reader as unlikely, since we have nothing remotely like it today, but a good deal of historical evidence supports this contention (Fideler 1993, 73).[4]

Two final examples serve to illustrate these concepts. According to Pythagoreans, the universe is both One and Many. The beautiful *kosmos* represents a dynamic, harmonic union of the two ideal extremes of Unity and Diversity, Form and Matter, the Limited and the Unlimited elements.

In Pythagorean thought, these two fundamental poles of manifestation are represented by the numbers 1 and 2, the Monad and the Dyad. The Monad represents the Source of creation, the beginning and end of all things; the Dyad represents multiplicity, manifestation, division, duality, and the movement away from unity.

Two "opposing" terms need a third term, a principle of ratio or relation to bind them together. According to the Pythagoreans, the most perfect mediator between any two extremes is the geometric mean, which binds the two extremes together in a continued geometric proportion, as in A:B:C. Therefore, represented mathematically, the ideal principle of mediation between Unity and Multiplicity, between Spirit and Matter, between 1 and 2, is 2, for 1:2:2.

As can be seen from Fideler's diagram (see page 132 in this volume), $\sqrt{2}$ provides the number value of 1415, THE GOD APOLLO. Three-fourths of this value is 1061, APOLLO, while one-fourth of 1415 is HERMES, another representation of the Logos. In this diagram can be seen the actual source and primary symbolism of the key numbers of Greek gematria.[5]

The god Apollo is a representation of the ideal Logos (ratio), which links together Unity and Multiplicity, 1 and 2. Through the function of the Logos, unity may pass into multiplicity and multiplicity may return to unity. As the first and foremost manifestation of divine relation, THE GOD APOLLO, 1415, is by definition the First "Word" of Celestial Harmony (Fideler 1993, 214).

A final consideration concerns the symbolism of the Alpha and Omega, the First and the Last. The Greek letters alpha and omega symbolize the beginning (*arche*) and end (*telos*) of creation, the seed, and its manifestation. As a symbol of the First Cause, the word ALPHA, 532, is numerically equivalent to ATLAS, the figure in Greek mythology who "upholds the entire cosmos." Before the emergence of the "new song" of Christianity, it would appear that Apollo at Delphi was associated with the first and last mysteries (Fig. 2.6). He was the god of geometry and music, a personification of the Logos, and the first and last strings of his lyre were associated with the vowels "A" and "W." According to the Orphic *Hymn to Apollo*, he holds "the beginning (arche) and end (telos) to come" and "with your versatile lyre you harmonize the poles" (Fideler 1993, 272).

We have identified the god Hermes not only as the Trickster and the Lord of Words, but also as the Logos, a structure of mediation in the mathematical *harmonia* of Apollo. The archetypal orderedness we have encountered has prepared us for the next chapter in our story: "Plato's Cave and the Silver Screen."

2.6. Apollo with *cithara*, Apollo Citharoedus, believed to be a copy of Skopas. The cult image housed in the temple of Apollo Palatinus is also Apollo with a *cithara*

PLATO'S CAVE AND
THE SILVER SCREEN

*What if their prison had an echo which reached them in front
of them? Whenever one of the carriers passing behind the wall
spoke, would they not think that it was the shadow passing in
front of them which was talking? Do you agree?*

By Zeus I do.

*Altogether then, I said, such men would believe the truth to
be nothing else than the shadows of the artifacts? They must
believe that.*

—Plato, *The Republic*, trans. Grube

*Film gives simultaneously the effect of an actual happening
and of a picture.*

—Rudolf Arnhem, *Film as Art*

Hermes the messenger helps us see the powerful archetypal connections
between magic, tricks, and technology (Davis 23). As both the messenger and as the trickster, Hermes might also be considered the patron
of the cinema. After all, the cinematic experience, it can be argued, is both a
physical and mental illusion, and whole schools of film criticism concerned with
epistemology, ontology, and aesthetics have debated this crucial point.[1] Take,
for example, the principle of "the persistence of vision," the fundamental phys-
iological phenomena at the root of the ability to experience cinematic motion.
Rapidly projected images on the screen cause overlapping retinal stimulation
in the eye, and the brain interprets the received images in one continuous flow;
we experience "the persistence of vision." Thus, the eye itself is tricked in a very
simple way by technology, one which Hermes would obviously approve. This
perceptual illusion is not unlike Plato's cave analogy in *The Republic* by which
humankind is tricked by the illusory nature of reality. In addition to persistence

of vision there is the "willing suspension of disbelief," which one employs in watching a movie. In *The Philosophy of Film*, Ian Jarvie writes, "Experiencing a movie we *allow* ourselves to be deceived; we *suspend*, as the cliché has it, our disbelief; we *play* with our sense of reality. In experiencing films people solve philosophical problems without thinking about them, thereby accomplishing what some philosophical theories do not" (Jarvie 31). In film-viewing, the suspension of disbelief is not the same as hallucination in which we take for real something that is not real and cannot tell the difference. It would seem with film-viewing that we are able to *play at* taking events onscreen for real. We learn not to be fooled as small children are, and we continue to enjoy movies despite no longer being fooled, even to the point of accepting the idea that onscreen characters will be fooled and fool us in ways we have learnt not to be. It is because of this playful distance that we become cognitively and affectively enthralled by movies (Jarvie 33). To participate in the cinematic experience is to invoke the Hermetic trickster.

In addition to the experience of the power of Hermes, watching and listening to films is an exact contemporary reenactment of the experience inside Plato's cave. This cinema-cave metaphor is an often-used cliché, perhaps, but significant in the context of this study of strong archetypal experience in the confrontation of symbols like the harp within the magically charged atmosphere of the cinema-cave (Fig. 3.1).

According to Geoffrey Hill:

Plato wrote a metaphorical story of some cave dwellers chained to the floor of their abode, only being able to see the shadows projected onto the wall before them. Being released from this colorless bondage, one can see brilliant varieties of colors and patterns in a whole new world of illuminated existence. Similarly, the first slide projector, called the magic

3.1. Plato's cave. We are reenacting Plato's thought experiment every time we experience a film. Ian Jarve, *Philosophy of the Film: Epistemology, Ontology, Aesthetics*, Routledge & Kegan Paul, New York and London, 1987

lantern, hints of its numinous characteristic of being able to project illuminated brilliant images onto a screen in a dark room (and thus into the human soul). In England, the cinema house was originally called the "bioscope," signifying the viewing of life. Indeed, in the cinema as in the theater of life, the screen of human existence casts illuminating shadows onto the wall of tribal participation. Film is the medium par excellence for conveying myth, whether or not, as Marshall McLuhan points out, the film in question transports the viewer to another world (Hill 15):

Whatever the camera turns to, the audience accepts. We are transported to another world. As René Clair observed, the screen opens its white door into a harem of beautiful visions and adolescent dreams, compared to which the loveliest real body seems defective. Yeats saw the movie as a world of Platonic ideals with the film projector playing "a spume upon a ghostly paradigm of things." (McLuhan 286)

Geoffrey Hill also writes, "When myths are manifested in film we see the emergence and continuation of particular genres that promote mass participation in each respective myth. According to analytical psychology each of us has stirring within us the symbols, archetypes, and myths of a vast collective unconscious inherited from ancestors of the distant and recent past. Through a familiarity with symbols, religion, and mythology, mythic connections can be found in even the most secular films, as in the most secular psyches" (Hill 14).

At this point in our discussion of the archetype of the harp in film, it is time for us to answer the question, "Exactly what are archetypes and symbols anyway and how does this relate to movies?"

Jolande Jacobi, writing of the nature of the archetype in *Complex Archetype and Symbol in the Psychology of C. G. Jung*, says no exact definition of Jung's concept of the archetype is possible. At best one can suggest its general implications by "talking around it." The archetype represents a profound riddle surpassing rational comprehension. Quoting Jung: "An archetypal content expresses itself, first and foremost, in metaphors; there is some part of its meaning that always remains unknown and defies formulation. No direct answer can be given to the questions of whence the archetype comes and whether or not it is acquired."

He continued: "Archetypes are, by definition, factors and motifs that arrange the psychic elements into certain images, characterized as archetypal, but in such a way that *they can be recognized only from the effects they produce*" (Jacobi 31). Jung writes that the unconscious, as the totality of all archetypes, is the deposit of all human experience right back to its remotest beginnings. Not, indeed, a dead deposit, a sort of abandoned rubbish heap, but a living system of reactions and aptitudes that determine the individual's life in invisible ways—all the more effective because invisible. It is not just an a priori historical condition; it is also the source of the instincts, for Jung held the archetypes are simply the forms, which the instincts assume.[2]

No archetype can be reduced to a simple formula. It is a vessel that we can never empty and never fill. It has a potential existence only, and like Plato's idea or form, when it takes shape in matter it is no longer what it was. Every archetype is capable of infinite development and differentiation; like a robust tree it can put forth myriad branches and many thousands of magnificent blossoms (Jacobi 55). The collective unconscious as suprapersonal matrix, as the unlimited sum of fundamental psychic conditions accumulated over millions of years, is a realm of immeasurable breadth and depth. From the very beginning of its development, it is the inner equivalent of Creation, an inner cosmos as infinite as the cosmos outside us is infinite (Jacobi 59). The archetype, when it becomes perceptible to the conscious mind, is *the introspectively recognizable form of a priori psychic orderedness*. It may be regarded as an organizer of representations, working outward from within the unconscious as a kind of DNA or organizing principle. In comparison with our individual temporality, the life of the archetype is timeless and limitless (Jacobi 64).

When the archetype manifests itself in the here and now of space and time, it can be perceived in some form by the conscious mind. This is when we speak of a *symbol*, and every symbol is at the same time an archetype. In order to appear as a symbol, the archetype must have an "archetypal ground plan." But an archetype is not identical with a symbol. It is an invisible center of energy, always a potential symbol, and whenever a general psychic constellation, a suitable situation of consciousness, is present, its dynamic nucleus is *ready to actualize itself and manifest itself as a symbol*. In other words, the archetype is concentrated psychic energy, and the symbol provides the mode of manifestation by which the archetype becomes discernible. In this sense, Jung defines the symbol as the "essence and image" of psychic energy. Consequently, one can never encounter the archetype as such *directly*, but *only indirectly*, when it is manifested in the archetypal image as a symbol. As long as something is unconscious, no statement can be made about it; hence any statement about the archetype is only an inference. A symbol is never entirely abstract, but always in some way "incarnated" (Jacobi 75–76).[3]

In Chapter I of this study, we saw that the harp is one of the oldest musical instruments developed at the dawn of civilization by humankind. As such, it is an apt example of the evolution or development of an archetypal symbol. The harp, aka "Hermes's Joke," has become more than a musical device or a decorative accessory. As it has evolved through three thousand years of culture and mythology it has become a symbol with considerable archetypal power.

With this in mind, it is now time to answer the questions posed in the introduction of this study: What is the subtext of Harpo Marx's transforming harp performances? And, moreover, why is Cary Grant playing a harp in *The Bishop's*

Wife; why was there a harp in the living room of Miss Thanatogenos in *The Loved One*; or a gold concert harp in the back of a wagon fleeing Atlanta in *Gone with the Wind*; why was there an equally ornate harp in President Martin Van Buren's White House in *Amistad*; or in the Fifth Avenue apartment of Woody Allen's *Small Time Crooks*; and what were all those female human-harps doing in the Busby Berkeley dance number in *Fashions of 1934*; why was there a harp in the bedroom seduction scene in *Bedazzled*; and, finally, what was meaning of the harp in the chamber with "Fluffy" in the first blockbuster *Harry Potter* film?

If Marshall McLuhan is correct in arguing that each of our media is an extension of ourselves, and that the medium is the message, then his argument must contend that film is but an extension of our most inward and most ancient consciousness. After successive epochs of civilization, through a long and circuitous route, the numinous soul now extends and manifests itself through film, but this spiritual element endemic to film still conveys human expression at its most primitive state, despite our use of highly sophisticated technology (Hill 19).

> While the primitives have their rituals, possessions, medicines, and incantations (which we also have in various forms) we as moderns have our movie house. The movie house is the perfect place for such haunting. The dark cavern of the cinema is reminiscent of a ceremonial sweat lodge, an initiation pit, the dark night of the soul, the belly of the fish, the alchemical grave, or the wilderness of the night journey. The movie house is the tomb of our rational consciousness and the womb of our conversional rebirth. It is the communal meeting place where tribal strangers of like mind meet to explore the inner reaches of the soul. It is the baptismal font where our skepticism is drowned in the motherly sea of awe and wonder. It is the renewal of Plato's cave, where we are allowed a glimpse of the other side. It is our temple, our shrine, our house of worship, and our prayer room. It is a psychoanalytic depth chamber and a tribal rallying hall.
>
> Depending on our level of suspended disbelief, we all participate at different levels, but we all participate. The primitive and naive participate in the witch doctor's magic wholeheartedly, and the modern sophisticates participate with guarded mind and denial, but we all participate. (Hill 20-21)

So now let us enter the cave and commune with the instrument of Hermes the Trickster.

4.1. "Welcome to Hell," © 1986 Gary Larson, FarWorks, Inc., Dist. by Andrews McMeel Syndication. All rights reserved.

IV

THE HEAVENLY INSTRUMENT

*When he took it, the four living creatures and the twenty-four
elders fell down before the Lamb. Each of the elders had a harp,
and they held golden bowls full of incense, the prayers of God's
people, and they were singing a new song.... Then as I looked
I heard the voices of countless angels. These were all round the
throne and the living creatures and the elders. Myriads upon
myriads there were, thousands upon thousands crying aloud.*

—Revelation 5: 8, 11

There's a wonderful drawing by Gary Larson, the creator of *The Far Side* cartoon series, which depicts two scenes: The first depicts deceased souls arriving at the entrance to Heaven where an angel is handing out harps with the greeting, "Welcome to heaven ... Here's your harp." In the second scene, the souls of the damned arrive in Hades where the Devil greets them with, "Welcome to hell ... Here's your accordion." This humorous scene aptly describes the image of the harp for many people (Fig. 4.1). Popular culture has routinely depicted winged angels in gossamer robes carrying gold harps surrounded by the clouds of paradise. It is not without good reason that no other musical instrument has been so romanticized, accordions and "Lady of Spain" notwithstanding, as "the heavenly instrument."

In Chapter I, if you recall, the harp and organ were the only instruments to survive from classical times into the Middle Ages and this was no doubt because of their acceptance by the Christian Church. When at last the organ found its way into the churches it was used to accompany vocal and not instrumental music. The instruments of antiquity were seen only in the hands of loose women and clowns. On the other hand, all the instruments of the Old Testament (and especially the harp of David) were regarded with exceptional respect, even if nobody had ever seen them (Buchner 16).

Previously, I mentioned the illuminated twelfth-century English manuscript in which Alexander Buchner describes those instruments permitted by the Church and those others that the Church condemned, thus contrasting God's musicians and the Devil's music-makers.

Within Christian scripture, there are three references to the harp (or what would traditionally be interpreted as the harp) that the church embraced in its traditions, producing these themes, which appear throughout Western European religious art, sculpture, painting, and architecture. In fact, it is through the harp's mostly accurate depiction in ecclesiastical art that we have the only visual evidence for many of the instrument's early forms. These three references involved King David, the Tree of Jesse, and the Twenty-Four Elders.

All Christianity knows the biblical story of David, the shepherd boy, and his encounter with King Saul, writes author Hans Zingel. David's role as a psalmist and singer is familiar, too, and everyone knows that the Old Testament figure is represented playing the harp (Zingel 59). David is indeed one of the most popular figures in the Bible, and the Church viewed him as the link to Jesus in the New Testament (Fig. 4.2). This is very significant as we recall the metamorphosis of the Greek hero, Orpheus, "the good shepherd," into King David. The Hermetic image of the "pymander" or shepherd passed into the Old Testament mythology and resurfaced in the Gospel references to Jesus. Artists usually represented David playing a harp rather than a lyre and for good reason. The instrument referred to as a harp is said to be "sounding from above," which means that it responded to inspiration from supernatural regions. Of the lyre, exactly the opposite was said. The difference of attitude towards the two instruments is sufficient to explain how the harp came to be regarded as sacred and associated with David (Zingel 60). We recall from the discussion of harps in the ancient world that the form of the harp had the soundbox above the strings while the instrument is being played. Therefore, writes Zingel, one may well say that the sound comes from above. The Near Eastern angular harp was the most widespread and highly perfected form of the instrument at the time of the birth of Christ. At the time when the harp, as far as its structure was concerned, had nothing more in common with the Near Eastern instrument, its allegorical significance in theology was unchanged and the harp became a stock symbol. Artists began to depict David playing the form of harp that was popular at the time. The fact that a tuning key is shown so often has an allegorical significance in addition to a technical one: David is regarded as the keeper of order in the realm of sounds and is thus responsible in a general way for proper tuning of the intervals. David's importance was manifold: he was a poet and singer of the psalms, he was regarded as the patron of music, he was a king, and he had the task of keeping order in the acoustic world (Zingel 61). For Christians, Hermes has become David (Fig. 4.3).

The figure of David was so familiar to all Christians that they were able to recognize it among a crowd of other figures in a representation of "all saints."

4.2. *David Playing the Harp*, psalter of Westminster Abbey, c. 1200 AD, Royal Manuscript collection, postcard, the British Library

4.3. King David with harp, close-up of north window, Chartres Cathedral, thirteenth century, postcard, Chartres Cathedral, France

The same applies to the rows of figures to be seen in Gothic cathedrals. David, always recognizable from his attributes, appears among other kings, patriarchs, and prophets of the Old Testament (Zingel 64).

That David was seen as the ancestor of Christ brings up the second reference, which endeared the harp to the Church and Christian iconography, namely the Tree of Jesse. This much-favored theme in Gothic sculpture and stained-glass window designs as well as in manuscript illuminations provided another opportunity to represent King David with the harp. The specific identity of the other biblical figures on the Tree is now vague, but the harp (even incorrectly played) ensures immediate recognition of the psalmist King (Rensch 62).

The final source for the harp's divine image comes from representations of the Twenty-Four Elders, which were especially popular for church facade decoration in the latter part of the twelfth century. This theme provided sculptors with an opportunity to carve a variety of musical instruments, and various forms of harps can be seen. The concept of the Twenty-Four Elders is a reference to the Book of Revelations, chapter 5, verse 8, which is quoted at the beginning of this chapter. The Twenty-Four Elders bow down to the Lamb of God and each is holding a harp. The significance of the number twenty-four relates to the hours of the day and office of worship. The design of the great rose

4.4. Great Rose Window at Durham Cathedral, originally glazed in the fifteenth century by Richard Pickering. The present glass dates from the late nineteenth century and depicts Christ surrounded by the apostles, in turn surrounded by the Twenty-Four Elders from Revelation. Note that all Twenty-Four Elders are holding harps. Durham Cathedral and Jarold Printing

window behind the High Altar at Durham Cathedral in England is based on this passage. The window is divided into twenty-four sections for the hours of the day and in each section, there is a medallion depicting various saints, each holding a harp (Fig. 4.4).

The source of the praise and worship tradition flows from Psalm 150:3: "Praise him with the sound of the trumpet: praise him with the psaltery and the harp." In the seventeenth century, hymnals and psalters were often figuratively titled "the Harp of David." In the lengthy preface to one of these publications it is said that "the divine harpist, whomsoever he is absorbed in religious contemplation, may be carried aloft to join the band at the court of the Almighty and to sing the praises of God with the ascending Seraphim."

The Church thus apotheosized the harp of David (and Hermes/Orpheus) from scriptural sources, and it became the instrument of the angels. The word "angel," αγγελοσ in Greek, *malak* in Hebrew, literally signifies a "person sent" or a "messenger," according to author Lewis Spence. It is a name, not of nature, but of office, and is applied also to men in the world, as ambassadors or representatives. In Revelation, a vast idea of their number is given. They are called the "armies" of heaven. Their song of praise is described as "the voice of a great multitude, and as the voice of many waters, and as the voice of many thunderings." As to their nature, it is essentially the same as that of man, for not only are understanding and will attributed to them, but they have been mistaken for men when they appeared, and Paul represents them as capable of disobedience. There is nothing in the whole of scripture to say that intelligent beings exist who have other than human attributes. The division of angels into nine orders or three hierarchies, as derived from Dionysius the pseudo-Areopagus, was held in the Middle Ages, and gave the prevalent character to much of their symbolism. The Christian fathers, for the most part, believed that angels possessed bodies of heavenly substance (Tertullian calls it "angelified flesh") and could assume a corporeal presence at their pleasure. In fact, all the actions recorded of them in scripture suppose human members and attributes (Spence 24-26).

Harold Bloom, writing in *Omens of Millennium*, states that angels are anything but ephemeral images. The historical sequence of Western religions—Zoroastrianism, Judaism, Christianity, Islam—has not known how to tell the story of their truths without angelic intercessions, nor is there any major religious tradition, Eastern or Western, that does not rely upon angels (Bloom 37). Though the Bible's angels, like the Koran's, appear to be males only, the older tradition in Persia and Babylonia stressed the existence of female angels as well. For John Milton, angels were a mirror into which all of us gaze and behold neither ourselves nor an absolute otherness, but a middle region where self and other mingle (Bloom 39).

The great insight from Thomas Aquinas is that angels have perfect knowledge of their own spirituality and so of their own freedom. We stumble about, knowing nothing but facts, while the angels are great Platonists, as it were, and know the Ideas directly, yet also know all the facts (Bloom 55).

In the 1947 film *The Bishop's Wife*, starring Cary Grant; the 1950 film *For Heaven's Sake*; and the 1954 film *The Angel Who Pawned Her Harp*, the plotlines revolve around an angel character on a mission, who interacts with the other characters and thereby causes some type of transformation. Numerous visual tricks are played, such as appearing, disappearing, and walking through solid doors and walls. Both angels are men, Cary Grant and Clifton Webb, and appear as ordinary human characters like Clark Kent in the Superman series. Not surprisingly, both are also proficient on the harp!

In *The Bishop's Wife*, we are treated to a harp solo by Cary Grant, whose hands are skillfully replaced in the shot by the nimble fingers of Hollywood harpist Gayle Laughton. Grant beams professionally as his hands appear to glide up and down the strings with numerous glissandos and arpeggios (Fig. 4.5). The "trick" is apparently successful, as the character to whom this performance is directed, a wealthy benefactor, experiences an inner transformation and reverses her decision not to endow the cathedral parish Grant has come to rescue. Grant, of course, plays the beneficent visitor, Dudley, who soothes the neglected feelings of the wife (Loretta Young) of a distraught bishop

Screenshots from *The Bishop's Wife*, Samuel Goldwyn/Warner Bros., 1947

Clockwise from top left:

4.5. The Angel (Cary Grant) examining the harp in the living room of his patron.

4.6. Cary Grant seated at a pedal harp as a modern-day angel.

4.7. Cary Grant beams professionally as his "hands" (supplied by Hollywood harpist Gayle Laughton) glide skillfully along the strings.

played by David Niven, who has lost sight of his priorities in his determination to build a cathedral (Fig. 4.6). Dudley has come to assist the bishop in his project and to straighten things out spiritually. In addition to many subtle supernatural acts that he performs in his role as the assistant to the bishop, Dudley also manages to perform a major ice-skating routine (also dubbed by an unknown professional) in addition to his convincing harp solo, which is casually tossed off to impress a rich benefactor of the church. In the harp routine, Dudley plays from a secret score that only his wealthy patron has knowledge of. It was written for her by her late husband as a love token, and she had hidden it away. The shock of seeing and hearing Dudley bringing the music to life on the harp in her living room results in a major transformation and conversion in her character (Fig. 4.7). Dudley's actions move the plot forward as misunderstandings resolve themselves and priorities get reestablished. In the end, the bishop realizes the spiritual and emotional distraction caused by his cathedral project and is reunited with his wife. Dudley plays the part of a kindly counselor or psychiatrist who steps in to affect changes in the characters. No one recognizes him as an angel, even though he tells the bishop that he has come in response to the bishop's prayers for help and guidance.

In George Seaton's 1950 heavenly comedy, *For Heaven's Sake*, there is a very funny performance by Clifton Webb as an angel (Charles) who comes to Earth

Screenshots from *For Heaven's Sake*, Twentieth Century Fox, 1950

top left: 4.8. Clifton Webb as an angel (invisible to seated Robert Cummings) casts a disparaging eye at the gold harp that is used as a decorative accessory by the wife of Cummings's character.

top right: 4.9. Webb argues with his fellow angel about how to accomplish their mission of causing the couple to fall in love. Webb's character can't resist playing a harp in his spare time.

middle: 4.10. Clifton Webb seated at the harp, which he plays for the couple to whom he was assigned from heaven.

bottom: 4.11. While playing some new jazz pieces he learned on his earthly mission, Webb shows his flair to a hotel staff member who wiggles out of the room in time to Webb's music.

to help an overly busy couple, played by Robert Cummings and Joan Bennett, have a baby (Figs. 4.8-4.9). Cummings and Bennett have little to do but Webb gives a fine comic performance. In one scene, he is in his hotel room playing a rather cheerful jazz number on the pedal harp (Fig. 4.10). It's a music style he has picked up while on Earth, in contrast to what he is accustomed to playing in heaven. Jazz harp music was new for the 1950s and Webb does a fairly accurate job fingering the harp strings. While playing away at the harp, the room-service waiter arrives with a dinner cart (Fig. 4.11). Webb keeps on playing while the waiter makes his delivery, receives his tip, and wiggles out the door in time to the harp music.

In both examples, the harp is clearly associated with angelic visitors who also happen to be male. In the last example, the angelic visitor is a woman, and

Screenshots from *The Angel Who Pawned Her Harp*, directed by Alan Bromly, 1954, Group 3 Ltd., UK

Clockwise from top right:

4.12. The angel (Diane Cilento) appears in the pawn shop with her harp as collateral for a loan.

4.13. Local children mesmerized by her harp playing.

4.14. Pawn shop owner (Felix Alymer) negotiates the value of the pawned harp with a musical instrument dealer.

4.15. The angel plays for the shop owner (Felix Alymer) and an Irish buddy who suspects, with no proof, that the harpist is an angel. As she plays, they fall into a trance and awaken with changed attitudes about their problems.

the plot resembles the previous two: a heavenly visitor comes to Earth and is assigned a mission to assist several mortals in their personal conflicts. In the British film *The Angel Who Pawned her Harp* (1954), beautiful blond actress Diane Cilento plays an angel who has been assigned a mission to help Londoners find their way to happiness. She finds herself in Islington in London, with no money and only her pedal harp. So she approaches a pawnshop to see if she can receive a loan for her instrument (Fig. 4.12). The shop owner (Felix Aylmer) is a world-class collector of music boxes, and his shop assistant is one of the individuals that she has been assigned to assist. The plot revolves around him and several folks in the neighborhood, but the object at the center is the angel's harp, which moves in and out of the plot and the pawnshop. Cilento plays several short numbers on the instrument, each of which enchants the listeners (Fig. 4.13). Magically their previous attitudes are altered following her performance. Hermes strikes again(!) (Fig. 4.14).

Cilento uses some of her pawn money to play the dog races to increase her holdings. At first, she is wildly successful, tripling her investment, and is able to buy back her harp before the shop owner is able to sell it (Fig. 4.15). She manages to solve all of her assigned cases of helping before being recalled to Paradise, but she forgets to retrieve her beloved harp. The film was favorably received. A reviewer on the Rotten Tomatoes website commented, "A gentle and moving film, weaving elements of sentiment and ingenuity, fantasy and realism, into a very entertaining package!" It is interesting to note that Cilento was for many years married to Sean Connery. The film was based on a novel by Charles Terrot and is a remake of a television play written by him and broadcast in 1951. It was remade as a West German film of the same title in 1959.

The idea of heaven naturally brings to mind the concept of immortality, death and transcendence. In the next chapter, we will see how the harp in film has related to these broader themes.

V

TRANSCENDENCE

Into the audience hall by the fathomless abyss where
Swells up the music of toneless strings I shall take this
Harp of my life.
I shall tune it to the notes of forever, and, where it
has sobbed out its last utterance, lay down my silent
Harp at the feet of the silent.

—Rabindranath Tagore, 1861–1941

And whenever the spirit from God troubled Saul, David took the
harp and played: then Saul grew calm, and recovered, and the
evil spirit left him.

—I Samuel 16:23

As we have seen, the harp became a stock symbol for the angelic realms early in the history of the church. Such association implies a connection with death as reflected in the *Far Side* cartoon. There is a very funny scene in Tony Richardson's 1965 black comedy *The Loved One*, which was billed as a film "with something to offend everyone." The film is filled with jokes about death, love, sex, capitalism, religion, and poetry. Ultimately it was a send-up of Forest Lawn and the Hollywood funeral industry.

Newly arrived in Hollywood from England, Dennis Barlow (Robert Morse) finds he must arrange his uncle's interment at the highly organized and profitable Whispering Glade memorial park. His fancy is caught by an aspiring cosmetician, Aimee Thanatogenos, and he finally persuades her to allow him to visit her at home. When he arrives, he discovers that she lives in a condemned dwelling precariously perched on the side of a cliff, which has frequent landslides (Fig. 5.1). Aimee seems totally unconcerned and keeps removing the condemnation notices posted by the city.

In the center of her living room amid a collection of crystal knickknacks and *objets d'art* stands a gold pedal harp. As Dennis looks nervously about, Aimee

Screenshots from *The Loved One*, MGM, 1965

5.1. Dennis Barlow (Robert Morse) arrives at the condemned house of Aimee Thanatogenos (Anjanette Comer), which is dangerously perched on a cliff.

5.2. *"You see, Dennis, I like to surround myself with beauty,"* says Aimee Thanatogenos, caressing the harp.

5.3. *"But isn't this place liable to fall down?"* asks Dennis as the house shakes.

says, caressing the harp, "You see, Dennis, I like to surround myself with beauty, while others are concerned with comfort" (Fig. 5.2). "But isn't this place liable to fall down?" he asks. "Yes, I suppose it is," she replies, then retires to the deck where she seats herself in a swing and begins to swing herself out over the canyon below. "Isn't it enchanting?" she says. "It's absolutely breathtaking," he whispers nervously, having tottered by the harp and spying the gaping holes in the deck (Fig. 5.3). "You know; some people think of death as . . . a negative thing," she continues, "but you see how wrong they are, don't you? What could be more beautiful and more thrilling than eternal rest! You do love beauty don't you?" The house shakes again. Dennis: "What's that?" "Oh, that's just another rockslide!" she replies casually.

5.4. David (Iro Payer) plays for King Saul (Orson Wells), *David and Goliath*, Allied Artists, 1961, screenshot

Reviewer Stephen Brophy of *The Tech* at MIT wrote, "'Loved one' is a euphemism for a corpse used by the various functionaries of an ostentatious cemetery in Los Angeles, c. 1965. It was a cemetery dreamed up by Evelyn Waugh (*Brideshead Revisited*) after spending a few weeks in Hollywood. Most of the characters are caricatures, wickedly drawn and uniformly well-acted" (Brophy 9). What could be more morbidly evocative than a harp in the center of an ersatz Victorian parlor of a house about to collapse and slide down a mountain?

On a less morbid note, the music of the harp has transcendent qualities. The 1961 version of *David and Goliath* depicts the scene in which King Saul brings David, the young shepherd boy, to his court to play the harp and soothe his disposition. Faithful to the text, the film has David (Iro Payer) kneeling by Saul (Orson Welles) playing an arched harp (Fig. 5.4). In usual Hollywood style, a concert harp replaces the twanging strings; nevertheless, Saul is entranced. *David and Goliath* is in the "sword and sandal" genre and follows the biblical narrative closely. Its English dialogue is ponderous, often unintentionally humorous as the characters speak to each other in King James English.

Another transcendent image of the harp appears in *The Aristocats*. This 1970 Disney animated film is directed by Wolfgang Reitherman, who was an animator on many classic Disney films, including *Fantasia, Dumbo*, and *Lady and the Tramp*. The plot is a variation of *Lady and the Tramp*, only set in Paris at the turn of the century. A family of well-to-do cats stand to inherit the fortune of their elderly human mistress. The butler, upon overhearing her plan, manages to kidnap the cats and have them dumped far in the countryside so he will inherit the estate.

The plot becomes an adventure story as the abducted aristocats attempt to get back home. The charming Thomas O'Malley, a rough-and-tumble alley cat, saunters by and offers to escort them home. Along the way, they stop at Thomas's "pad," where a group of alley cats are jamming. Scat Cat and his band of swingin' jazz cats perform the popular "Ev'rybody Wants to Be a Cat."

Screenshots from *The Aristocats*, Disney, 1970

Clockwise from top left:

5.5. Duchess, the high-society cat, and her three kittens join in a jam session with other outcast cats in Paris. In a break in the raucous music, she seats herself at a dilapidated harp and draws in the audience with her musical talent.

5.6. Duchess pulls the strings of the harp.

5.7. An entranced admirer on the soundboard.

Amid this musical number, Duchess, the mother, seats herself at an old harp and begins to play (Fig. 5.5). Immediately, the band pauses with everyone sighing and listening dreamily to the harp interlude. It's almost like Harpo Marx's solos. As Duchess plays, all the members of the band (mostly male) pause, and each is transported to another level of dreamy bliss. Then the music swings back into a fast rhythm and the band resumes its wild jazzy pace (Figs. 5.6–5.7).

A final example of the harp as an image of the transcendent occurs in Jean Cocteau's 1930 film, *Blood of A Poet (Le sang d'un poete)*. Cocteau's first feature is a highly personal, poetic, symbolic fantasy, which supposedly transpires in a split second, the time it takes for a chimney to crumble and fall.

Cocteau described his first film as a disturbing series of voyeuristic tableaux, as "a descent into oneself, a way of using the mechanism of the dream without sleeping." *Blood of a Poet* was based on his private mythology. Dennis Schwartz writes that typical of Cocteau's films was the use of mirrors as a door into another world and the play between reality and the underworld of the inner world where poetry is made. The film is a work on the nature of creating art. In the first part, the artist struggles to find his identity, vowing to free himself

 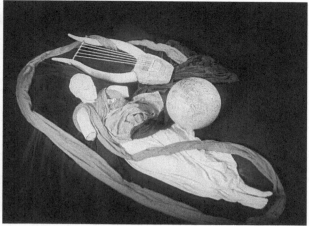

Screenshots from *Blood of a Poet*, Jean Cocteau, Janus Films, 1930

5.8. "The mortal tedium of immortality." A female statue carries a globe and a lyre to the grave.

5.9. "Only the poet is eternal."

from his present confinement by becoming a martyr for his art. He symbolically kills himself to attain a new relationship to tradition (Schwartz 3).

In the fourth and final episode, titled "Stolen Card," an artist commits suicide at a card table, a reminder that Cocteau's father committed suicide and of Cocteau's artist friends who live an impoverished life and are forced to make life-and-death decisions. The film ends with the message: the mortal tedium of immortality. Here the female statue, animated in the earlier episodes, carries a lyre and a world globe to the grave. There is an extended close-up shot of the lyre and the film ends with the caption "The mortal tedium of immortality" and returns to the opening shot of a chimney collapsing. The lyre is thus a symbol for transcendence (Figs. 5.8–5.9). As all material things are crushed only the poet remains and is considered eternal. Schwartz writes, "Because of its unusual theme and style and unpredictability, this is a film that deserves the high accolades many film critics have bestowed upon it. It resolutely shows how the filmmaker communicates into the spirit world, and he does so without being pretentious" (Schwartz 5).

The notion that "only the poet is eternal" takes us to the next part of this study of the harp: "The Bardic and Oracular Tradition."

VI

THE BARDIC AND ORACULAR TRADITION

Among the Celts are honored poets called bards who to the
music of harps (instruments like lyres) chant praise of some,
satire of others. Also they have philosophers called druids whom
they hold in high veneration. Prophets they have also who
foretell future events.

—Diodorus Siculus (c. 60 BC)

There is an axiom in musicology that states that all music is subordinate to the human voice. In other words, the human voice is the first musical instrument. According to *The Book of Music*, music for voices has its origins in religious rites. It was recognized from the earliest times that an enhanced form of speech could add a magical quality to the human voice. In ancient Greece, various devices were used to make the human voice both "magical" and more audible in a sacred context. The prophecies of the oracle were produced by means of a rock formation that acted as a megaphone, and the actors of Greek drama—primarily a religious activity—used masks to magnify and alter their voices (Rowley 56).

In Chapter I, we saw that primitive music was used for magical purposes; it was not made to provide pleasure and aesthetic enjoyment but was used to help man in his struggle against the overwhelming forces of nature. There were strong taboos against the unauthorized touching of musical instruments (Geiringer 29). Music chased the demons from Saul's soul when David played for him, and musical ecstasy took possession of the seers so that the spirit of God came upon them and made them prophesy (Sachs 105).

Barry Powell writes that human beings have told stories from time immemorial. Stories are a natural product of spoken language, an outgrowth of the imaginative powers. In societies that do not use writing, stories must be handed on by word of mouth, so traditional tales are the vehicle for the transmission of one generation's thought to another. In this way, traditional tales maintain

6.1. In the great hall of a Mycenaean palace, members of a royal household gather around the hearth to listen as a bard strums his lyre and sings epic lays about great heroes and their deeds. Illustration based on the great hall of the palace of Pylos, home of King Nestor, sage councilor of the Greek armies in the Trojan War. *The Epic of Man*, editors of *Life*, Time Inc., New York, 1961

contact with the past and pass inherited wisdom on to the future (Powell 3). A natural development in storytelling was the use of song as a means of recitation. The variations of pitch and rhythm provided a mnemonic system for recalling past deeds in the words of a chant.

We recall that in addition to his role as trickster, Hermes was also a magician and the Homeric herald. Norman Brown writes that the role of the herald predated the era of Homeric kingship when it became subordinated to the king. The etymological meaning for the Greek word for "herald," κῆρυξ, is "expert sound-maker"; thus his function had to do with ceremonial "sound-making." But what does this mean? Brown claims that the etymology suggests the pre-Homeric herald had a functional affinity with the singer or bard (Brown 29). "Philologists have concluded that the origins of song and poetry lie in the intoned formulae of magical incantations. . . . Thus the two crafts of the herald and the bard seem to have been derived from the single craft of the leader in magic ritual" (Brown 30).

In the *Iliad* and *Odyssey*, music-making was a high position in Homeric society and was not given over to slaves (Maas 5). Aside from Apollo, all the players described in the Homeric poems are either respected professional *aoidoi* ("singers") who were always male and who earned their living through their craft, or male amateurs such as Achilles or Paris (Fig. 6.1). The two chief bards in the *Odyssey*, Phemios and Demodokos, are clearly members of the class of professionals. Demodokos, the blind singer at the Phaiakian court of Alkinoos, may be the prototype for the notion of Homer as a blind poet. Blindness would have been no particular handicap in a tradition of oral poetry, and indeed, might even have increased one's capacity for the concentration necessary for such an art (Maas 5).[1]

By the time of Homer, writes Brown, ritual exists without song, and song without ritual, and each has its own expert. During preclassical times, the *kithara* was an instrument of bards, who accompanied their epic songs on it, but by the classical age it had become that of professional players, the *kitharoedoi*.

In Britain, the earliest texts mentioning druids talk of the esteem in which poets were held, writes R. J. Stewart. It seems there was a formalized druidic or bardic philosophy commonly held throughout Britain from early years of the Christian era until the fifth or sixth century AD. The earliest bardic records date to about this time. As Christianity developed in Britain, druidry ceased gradually to be the dominant religion. The bards, however, continued to weld semi-druidical powers of blessing and cursing, praise, and satire, well into the Middle Ages. In Britain, the high bards are differentiated from lower ones as follows: high-degree bardic practice—*Prydyddiaeth*; family harper practice—*Teulwriaeth*; and traveling minstrel practice—*Clerwriaeth*. Bards of high degree in Britain were recognized as having undergone an initiation into the mysteries of the art under the patronage of the goddess Ceridwen. According to Stewart, the three things that make a bard are: playing the harp, knowledge of ancient lore, and poetic power (Stewart 26-28).

The harp is central to the whole Celtic notion of spoken-word performance and the whole idea of inspiration. All poetry was originally religious. Poetry was the first religion, says the ancient Greek author Strabo. Celtic poetry was intended to be chanted, declaimed, or sung to the harp. Ceremony, magic, and healing are to be understood as part of Celtic poetry and harp music (Stewart 35).

Robert Armstrong writes that the earliest notice of a harp player occurs about 541 BC. This person, Craftine, is mentioned in several legendary tales. Craftine, whose instrument has been injured, is stated to have gone to the woods in search of a suitable tree for the purpose of constructing another harp and the tree he selected was a willow. This means that the harp, when it was probably a small and primitive instrument, was constructed out of willow (Armstrong 2).

Willow is an interesting choice because it relates to the use of the harp in inspiring prophecy. In his article "The Oracular Nature of the Early Celtic Harp," Samuel Milligan writes of the curious practice of Celtic harp makers using two specific woods for the construction of harps to the virtual exclusion of all others. While other, better wood stocks were available, the preference was for willow and oak. Milligan argues that the ancient Celts were tree-worshippers, as reported by Julius Caesar, Pliny, and Tacitus. If the power of the gods were resident in the trees, then any object made of wood would assume a sacred character, varying in different woods depending on the deity concerned. Oak and willow were associated with divination and oracles. References to sacred and oracular uses of oak are many. Pliny noted that every sixth day of the lunar month the druids cut sacred mistletoe from the oak to infuse it in water as a remedy for various ills. Oak trees were known to attract lightning and until recently, Irish gypsies burned oak leaves to divine the future in the ashes. The word "druid" is thought to be derived from the word *derwydd* originally meaning an "oak man" or an "oak seer," the druids being particularly important as diviners and seers.

The willow was sacred to the triple or ninefold goddess, patroness of poetry and poetic wisdom. Since the goddess is so intimately connected with poetic inspiration, and since the willow tree is sacred to her, the use of willow wood in harp making would be fitting (Milligan 15-17).

The primary use of the harp was to furnish poetic inspiration. It will be recalled that in Chapter II, a reference was made to Hermes as the shamanistic boundary-crosser. Supernatural power was communicated to the bard through the sounds of the harp, and he would be inspired to prophesy, probably through the same sort of self-induced trance as utilized by the Apollonian priestess at Delphi, or the Sibyl at Cumae. Allusions to this practice appear in early sources. Such predictions would certainly be cast in poetic form, for poetry was sacred in its own right, and any holy man would be expected not only to deliver up his supernatural pronouncements in rhyme but equipped with interior metrical assonances as well (Milligan 14). As in most primitive societies, the early Celts protected sacred things with elaborate taboos, and remnants of these have survived. It was bad luck for a woman to touch a harp and until recently almost all harpists in Celtic countries have been men. The many instances of enchanted harps in folklore, harps that play by themselves without human hands, mysterious harp music heard in lonely or haunted places, and in general all the enchantment and mystery that the word "harp" can convey to the modern mind are logical survivals of this earlier belief that the instrument was a sacred and magical thing, and that its sacredness was based on its oracular use (Milligan 14).

Three films variously illustrate the bardic/oracular tradition of the harp: *The Robe* (1953), *Quo Vadis?* (1951), and *Darby O'Gill and the Little People* (1959). In the first two examples, both set in Rome in the first century AD, we see the use of the harp and lyre as we have discussed so far. Both films were major productions in their time and inspired many "sword and sandal" spinoffs. *The Robe* (1953) was the first CinemaScope production from Twentieth Century Fox, a shrewdly chosen vehicle to promote what became the most successful technical innovation in movie history, writes critic Glenn Erickson: "3-D and

Screenshots from *The Robe*, Twentieth Century Fox, 1953

6.2. Early Christians gather around to hear a lame singer, Miriam (Betta St. John), as she relates the version of a Gospel accompanied on her *kinnor*, the Hebrew version of a lyre.

6.3. Close up of Miriam (Betta St. John) relating the Gospel accompanied by her *kinnor* (lyre).

70mm have come and gone, but the anamorphic trick of squeezing a widescreen image onto a standard 35mm negative caught on big, due in no small part to *The Robe*'s success at the beginning" (Erickson 2).

The plot, based on the Lloyd Douglas novel, revolves around the tribune Marcellus Gallio (Richard Burton), who has been banished from Rome and arrives in Palestine after having offended the young Caligula by outbidding him for the slave Demetrius (Victor Mature). Marcellus is put in charge of the crucifixion of a Jewish rabbi sentenced by Pilate. In a dice game, he wins Jesus's robe, but thinks it bewitched when he is stricken with anxiety attacks after cloaking himself in it for a moment. He later returns to Rome a mental case where he breaks off his engagement to Diana (Jean Simmons).

An advisor to Emperor Tiberius suggests that to break the spell, Marcellus must return to Palestine and destroy the robe. In the Holy Land, he converts to Christianity under the tutelage of Justus and Simon Peter. Marcellus's second return to Rome puts him in a truly bad position as Caligula is now the emperor (Erickson, DVD Savant Review 2000).

We come upon the harp in a scene in which Marcellus, in seeking answers to his mental illness, encounters a community of early Christians in Jerusalem. A young lame woman named Miriam (Betta St. John) is chanting the Gospel story, recounting the life and wonders of Jesus to the accompaniment of a *kinnor*, the Jewish version of the lyre (Fig. 6.2). As she sings from her pallet, she plucks the strings, which are dubbed by a concert harp. However, in a most un-Hollywood fashion, there is only one note for each string and the tune is kept purposefully simple and quaint with only six notes. Her audience, a group of believers, remains transfixed as she recites her song of miracles. Marcellus is drawn in and later meets with the apostle Peter and his conversion begins. Here we have an example of the bardic tradition in the Homeric sense and in addition another example of the boundary-crossing use of the harp (Fig. 6.3).

A more elaborate (and campy) illustration is the 1951 blockbuster film *Quo Vadis?*, a glossy MGM extravaganza more pleasing to watch for its conspicuous opulence than for its dramatics, dialogue, or politics. "Directed with a mixture of tedium and oomph by Mervyn LeRoy. This Roman spectacle set in 64 AD, at the time of Nero's rule, runs for close to three hours before Nero decides to do the honorable thing and stick a knife in himself—which is his way to say he's done," writes critic Dennis Schwartz. The central plot revolves around a love story between Commanding General Marcus Vinicius (Robert Taylor) of the 14th Legion who has returned to Rome after three years in Britannia and a beautiful hostage named Lygia (Deborah Kerr) who is an early Christian. Marcus returns to a corrupt Rome under the twenty-nine-year-old Emperor Nero (Peter Ustinov), who killed his mother and his wife and loves to think of himself as an artistic soul, living a debauched life with harems and flatterers surrounding him as he plays a bad lyre and sings choppy verses to praise himself as a god greater than Jupiter. The plot concerns the romance between the Christian Lygia and the initially agnostic Roman commander Marcus who manages to get Nero to give her to him. Lygia resents Marcus but manages to fall in love with him despite his pagan status. Meanwhile, Nero acts on an unintentional suggestion of one of his courtiers, Petronius (Leo Genn) ("To write of it, you must live it, if you are a true artist") and has Rome set on fire in order to live his epic and create a new Rome of his own image, "Neropolis."

When blame is sought for the catastrophe, Nero's empress, Poppaea, suggests to him that he offer the explanation that the fire was started by the Christians. Thus, the Christians are rounded up and jailed for torture in the circus arena. Marcus and Lygia are also captured and jailed. But Nero's plans backfire as the army revolts after learning that Marcus has been arrested. When the populace learns that it was Nero who burned Rome, they turn on him and he commits suicide in the palace as the mob rushes in.

Screenshots from *Quo Vadis?* MGM, Loew's, Inc., 1951

6.4. Peter Ustinov as Emperor Nero reciting a song he is composing to his courtiers to the accompaniment of a rather ornate lyre in *Quo Vadis?*

6.5. "*Oh lamped flame,*" sings Nero (Peter Ustinov) as he plays his lyre before a court banquet, trying out his new song that he will later sing as Rome burns.

The main plot of *Quo Vadis?* deals with Roman persecution of the early Christians. The apostles Peter and Paul have minor roles. The film's title is Latin for "Where are you going, Lord?," referring to Peter's vision while fleeing Rome. The subtext behind Nero's lunacy is his fascination with being a "creative genius" who aspires to write an epic worthy of Homer or Vergil. His massive ego is manipulated by Petronius and Seneca so that he decides that in order to create an epic he must experience it. The burning of Rome serves as a background for Nero's experiential ravings.

The lyre appears in four important places in the story line. First, it introduces us to Nero's inner circle at the beginning of the film when he is rehearsing

Screenshots from *Quo Vadis?* MGM, Loew's, Inc., 1951

6.6. "*Sing ye gods,*" Nero (Peter Ustinov) sings his creation to the heavens as Rome is engulfed in flames. "*To know it, one must live it,*" Nero recites to his courtesans.

6.7. When Nero commits suicide with the help of his former mistress, Acte (Rosalie Crutchley), he falls dying on his lyre.

before a bored audience of courtiers (Fig. 6.4). Secondly, the same bad performance is repeated at an imperial banquet in honor of Marcus. The audience implores Nero to sing and, after feigned protests, he willingly obliges amid his cheering guests (Fig. 6.5).

The most famous scene occurs when Rome is flooded with fire except for the imperial grounds and Nero arrives on the palace roof to sing his great epic to the shock of his courtiers. Full of "divine inspiration," he attempts his lyrics as he presides over the flaming city, belting out poetry as if he were on the walls of Troy (Fig. 6.6). But the spectacle (or lack of it) overcomes him. When he spots an angry mob storming the palace reality sets in with more practical matters such as finding a scapegoat for the disaster. Nero has delusions of being a "boundary-crosser" but is aware he has been had by the trickster. Petronius addresses him sarcastically as "divinity," suggesting that since he was already a god, and therefore immortal, he should not fear the mob. Finally, at the end, when Nero, assisted by his faithful servant Acte, commits suicide, he tumbles across the floor; his lyre is pulled down and lands by his head and the sound of the strings is heard (Fig. 6.7).

The character of Nero provides us with the image of the debased *kithara* performer of the late classical period and its male player association. In an earlier, minor scene at the house of Petronius, the lovesick slave girl Eunice (Marina Berti) plays a harp (*pektis*) while her master plays a game of chess with Marcus. Here they are at home and the woman plays the harp. Worried, Petronius is brooding over Nero's unknown plans and comments to Eunice that even her beautiful playing cannot distract his thoughts from impending disaster (Fig. 6.8).

6.8. Petronius (Leo Genn) and Marcus Venicius (Robert Taylor) amuse themselves in Nero's court as they are being entertained by Petronius's Spanish slave girl (Mariana Berti) who is playing a *trigonon*.

6.9. From the lyre to the pedal harp. Peter Ustinov as Nero plucks his lyre with a studio harpist in this studio publicity shot. Possibly the harpist supplied the beautiful string sounds emanating from Ustinov's elegant cigar-box instrument. This studio sound practice always drives harp enthusiasts crazy.

Quo Vadis? was a box office success for MGM in the pre-CinemaScope era and was second only to *Gone with The Wind* in revenue. The Roman epic with a cast of thousands was the predecessor to *Ben-Hur* in 1959 and *Gladiator* in 2000.

The final example of the harp in the bardic and oracular tradition is in the 1959 Disney film *Darby O'Gill and the Little People*. This film could also fit into the chapter on comedy and fantasy; however, the archetypal elements point toward the Celtic tradition. Based upon H. T. Kavanaugh's folklore tales, this film has the added bonus of featuring a major pre–James Bond performance by Sean Connery. It's an Irish pastoral story that crosses a youthful romance with a humorous game of wits between an old man and a leprechaun. The story revolves around the lives of Darby O'Gill, the aging groundsman of Lord Fitzpatrick's summer house, his daughter Katy, and Michael McBride, the young replacement for Darby's job. In addition to this plot, on the supernatural front, there is also Darby's friendship with the wily King Brian of Knocknasheega, king of the leprechauns (the little people), who live in the mountain near the village. There are also more sinister notes, such as the banshee and the death coach, as well as the earthlier villain, the local bully Pony Sugrue.

After Darby finds that he is about to be replaced as the caretaker of the estate, he accidently falls down a well and finds himself in the kingdom of the leprechauns. He later captures the leprechaun king, Brian Connors, and keeps him imprisoned until Brian grants him three wishes with which he hopes to secure a future for himself and Katy.

In the scene where Darby comes to after falling down the well, he is discovered by two "little people" who escort him to the audience chamber of their king, Brian Connors. In the scene, the leprechauns are reveling in a huge cavern, which is the throne room. King Brian is playing a huge set of bagpipes (human-scale), and everyone is dancing wildly. Darby stands entranced at the scene. Then the king notices him and invites him to approach the throne. Darby remarks on the fine appointments and the king points out the various treasures surrounding his throne, which just happen to be the most archetypal treasures in Irish culture.

He invites Darby to have a seat on a chest overflowing with gold coins and jewels. "From the Spanish ships," the king mentions casually, "when the Armada wrecked on our coast. Got the ship's gun, too," he remarks, pointing to a large cannon beside the throne. "And the throne?" asks Darby. "By all the gods in Carrigafergus, man, do you think I would sit upon a Spanish throne?" the king asks indignantly. "This belonged to the ancient high king of Ireland, Fergus McCladducagh! And there's the cup of Ardagh," pointing to a huge chalice, "and here is the sword of Brian Boru who drove the Danes from Ireland, and over there is his harp!" Darby gasps and replies, "You don't mean the harp that once through Tara's Halls the soul of music shed?" "Ah, the very one!" There near the throne, propped up against a large stalagmite column is a bejeweled harp resembling the famous Brian Boru harp that appears on Irish coins (Fig. 6.10). "Oh wait till I tell the fellows down at the pub what I've seen!" Darby says. "Oh, you won't be needin' to worry about that," Brian says, "Once you're here, there's no going back!"

Darby suddenly realized he has been tricked by the king, who explains that he rescued Darby to escape the bad news that Lord Fitzpatrick was replacing him as groundsman on the estate. Darby is furious when the king says that

6.10. In the leprechauns' hall are the great treasures of Ireland including the harp of Brian Boru. Close-up of the Disney version of the Brian Boru harp with leprechauns playing it. *Darby O'Gill and the Little People,* Disney, 1959, screenshot

everyone will think Darby is dead and will give him a wake and forget about him. The king then asks Darby what he would like to do since he was there. "Would you like to have a hand at the harp?" "No, I'm not much good at the harp," he says. Then with a wink, "But I could do with a fiddle! I'll run right home and fetch mine!" as he starts out. But the king is too sharp and offers Darby a Stradivarius that was given to him in 1700 by the emperor of the Italian fairies. Darby takes the fiddle in hand and plays a mournful tune, then remarks, "There's three things that me grandfather told me the little people like best, dancin', whiskey, and hunting. So I'll give you a fox chase." He proceeds to play a fiddle tune in three parts, each one faster than the one before. The room is full of leprechauns, all little men in coattails with pointed hats, who begin to dance all around the room (Fig. 6.11). As the tempo increases the dancing gets wilder. There are several little people sitting and hanging on the harp and playing the strings. Then at the fox chase section of the tune, they bring out a large hunting horn, which the king blows. All the leprechauns rush out of the room and return each riding a miniature white horse. They swirl around the throne in a galloping circle (Fig. 6.12). Then the king gives a magic command and suddenly the side

Screenshots from *Darby O'Gill and the Little People*, Disney, 1959

6.11. Deep in the leprechauns' cave, Darby O'Gill (Albert Sharpe) plays a fiddle tune for the leprechauns—a fox chase—Darby's trick, which results in such excitement that they all rush out of the cave on tiny horses, leaving a narrow escape for Darby to follow them out through a magic hole in the mountain.

6.12. In a frenzy from Darby's fiddling, the leprechauns mount their horses and race out of the cave into the night leaving Darby an escape route.

of the cavern shudders and opens to the outside world. As Darby stands transfixed, the band of mounted leprechauns gallops through the opening and into the countryside. Darby, realizing he can escape, follows behind. Then remembering the jewels, he runs over to the chest and fills his pockets with gems. The cavern shudders and begins to close up again. Darby races to the entrance with jewels spilling from his coat pockets. He barely makes his escape as the wall closes up. Putting his hands in his pockets, he realizes all the jewels have fallen out and he has no proof of his magical experience with the little people. This was the major scene with the little people in the film. There are probably a hundred leprechauns in the shot (Fig. 6.12).[2]

The archetypal symbolism is unmistakable. In the scene are the three instruments that Celtic tradition says a person must master to gain entrance to heaven: the bagpipe, the harp, and the fiddle. Second, there is the trickster element. Darby and King Brian both work at trying to get the best of each other. The king used trickery to cause Darby to "cross the boundary" and fall down the well. Darby uses the trickery of the fiddle to escape by arousing the leprechauns into a fox chase, in which they race out of the cave. Throughout the film, Darby is the only character who can see the leprechauns. He brings the captured Brian into the pub in a canvas sack to prove he has not lost his mind and gives everyone a peep at the captured leprechaun. But all they see is a rabbit. When Darby looks in the bag, Brian waves innocently up to him. Everyone thinks Darby has finally lost his mind. Darby then holds a glass of port over the bag and the locals watch agog as it is taken from within and tossed back empty a moment later. The glass is then placed up on the shelf in case any local ever doubts. It's the perfect distillation of the barroom myths from which the leprechaun stories originated, writes Scheib. "The best thing in the whole film is the sly, shrewd performance from Albert Sharpe as Darby. With Popeye squint and a crusty rambunctiousness, he gets to run the entire gamut of a performance from shameless conman transparency to moving self-sacrifice" (Scheib, review, 1991).

As we have seen, in addition to magical qualities, there has been a gender association with forms of the harp since ancient times. We will examine these connections to sexuality in the next chapter.

USA WEEKEN...

Examine the uplifting, healing, transforming

Power of Music

We hear America singing. Join opera star Denyce Graves on a unique exploration of the science behind the sounds that soothe.

Plus: *"God Bless America, now more than ever"* by Irving Berlin's daughter

INSIDE: MARIA SHRIVER ON MAKING A DIFFERENCE • MEET THE NEW DARTH VADER

San Francisco Chronicle

7.1. Denyce Graves on the cover of *USA Weekend*, October 26, 2001, standing before two pedal harps for the cover article on "The Power of Music" by Tim Wendel. This issue came a month after the horrendous events of 9/11/2001 and focuses on the healing power of music. It is interesting that the photographer chose two harps to illustrate musical power. *USA Weekend Magazine*, San Francisco Chronicle, Gannett Co. Inc., 2001

VII

THE NAKED PIANO

The Harp appeals to the romantic nature of women, and indeed, there is no other instrument which so displays the charms of graceful femininity. Harp playing brings many opportunities for displaying the graceful movements of a pretty hand, arm and foot, to say nothing of the beautiful pose of the head, while the gold and artistic shape of the harp make an excellent foil for a beautiful gown.

—Melville Clark, *How to Play the Harp*, New York, G. Shirmer, 1932

Probably no other musical instrument has been so gender-identified as the harp. The harp is a sexy instrument, no doubt about it. The reason for this was explained in Chapter I. It is more than a naked piano; it reveals the soul of music. This was recently illustrated on the cover of *USA Weekend*, a tabloid insert in the Sunday edition of the *San Francisco Chronicle* (Oct. 26-28, 2001). The cover picture for the lead article, "The Power of Music" by Tim Wendel, featured mezzo-soprano Denyce Graves, who sang "America the Beautiful" at the National Cathedral in Washington only days after the September 11, 2001, attacks in Manhattan and at the Pentagon (Fig. 7.1). The article focused on the healing power of music in the wake of the September 11, 2001, national tragedy. The article also mentioned the connection between music and biology as discussed in the *New York Academy of Sciences Journal*, which had recently published an issue on *The Biological Foundations of Music* (see bibliography). The unusual thing about this article was the photo on the cover featuring Graves standing in front of two concert harps with her hands clasped to her breast as if she were nude. The picture says it all. The soul of music is revealed and stands naked before us. It's also sexy. Most people associate the instrument with a lovely female harpist, usually blond, stroking the strings. As we have seen in this study, it was not always so.

7.2. *A Song to Inspire*, nineteenth-century illustration of young woman playing the harp

7.3. Lyre-guitar, popular in the nineteenth century but died out as a historical curiosity

From earliest times until the nineteenth century, most harpers were men. The interesting exception was in the classical world where it will be recalled that the actual harp (*trigonon* or *pektis*) was played exclusively by women in private and the lyre and *kithara* were played by men. The bardic tradition was a male institution and men continued to be the chief performers until the decline of the clan system and the development of the pedal harp in the eighteenth century.

The single-action and double-action pedal harps were invented during the neoclassical Napoleonic period in Europe. The harp had become a parlor instrument and could take part in chamber music. It thus became a fitting accessory for the lady of leisure (Fig. 7.2). An early example of this trend shows up in the film *Dangerous Liaisons* (1988) in which a young lady (Uma Thurman) playing a harp is paired with a young suitor (Keanu Reeves) who plays the harpsichord in Georgian England (see Fig. 7.28).

The nineteenth century passion for classicism saw the final development in the form of the ancient *kithara*, before it passed into musical oblivion, ironically having been "feminized." By the Renaissance, the *kithara* had already evolved from the bowed *crwth* of the Middle Ages into the fretted instrument known as the guitar. But during the Napoleonic period the ancient form of the *kithara* was revived with the addition of a fretted neck attached from the soundbox to the yoke between the traditional curved arms. It was a guitar in a lyre shape; more precisely the neck and fretted strings of the true guitar were combined for the sake of appearance with the arms and crossbar of an ancient Greek or Roman lyre (Fig. 7.3). The appearance was immensely attractive, and the elegant shape, writes Lilly Stunzi, borrowed from antiquity, harmonized well with the flowing garb of the ladies at the courts of Vienna, Milan, and Naples, in Regency London and in the Paris Directoire (Stunzi 232). Today the lyre-guitar is but a musical

7.4. Nineteenth-century painting of three ladies in the harp salon

curiosity, yet it was the final stage in the evolution of the instrument of antiquity. Ironically, it expired as it was being embraced as a female instrument.

While the lyre-guitar may have become just another musical dodo, the pedal harp became extremely popular and more elaborately ornamented. The new pedal harp found its greatest success in Paris where, in the latter part of the eighteenth century, it had been taken up by members of the French court and fashionable society (Fig. 7.4). The future queen, Marie Antoinette (1755-1793), was already a harpist when she came to France in 1770 (Rensch 154-155). Whatever the extent of Marie Antoinette's harp playing, her interest in the instrument could only enhance its status since the French court set the standard for the courts of Europe, as well for French society (Rensch 158). Established at the French court, the pedal harp held its place during Napoleon's First Empire as well. According to Rensch, both the Empress Josephine and her daughter, Hortense, queen of Holland, took harp lessons in the music room at Malmaison, where the thirty-nine-string Cousineau harp made for the empress is still prominently on display (Rensch 162).

In Ireland, the feminization of the harp had begun when the harp appeared as a heraldic device under Charles I. As mentioned in Chapter I, the angelic female form of the harp borrowed from Celtic folklore became a stock symbol for Ireland. This image later appeared in folk tales like "Jack and the Beanstalk."

The harp gained popularity as an instrument favored by women throughout the eighteenth and nineteenth centuries. The instrument, due to its successful technical developments in becoming truly chromatic, however, had become more difficult to play for the amateur. When Melville Clark first introduced his small non-pedal harp in 1912, he wrote an accompanying instruction book clearly aimed at the female market. In his introduction (a part of which is quoted at the beginning of this chapter) Clark writes the following:

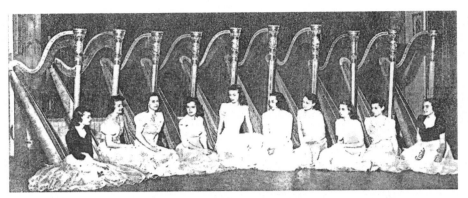

7.5. Harp ensemble at Oberlin College, early 1950s. Not a male in sight. Private collection

> While the harp in ancient times was played mostly by men, it is now attracting the attention of the most cultured and fashionable women. In New York alone at the present time there are hundreds of social leaders and women of fashion who are proficient players. In Europe there are several ladies of the nobility who are enthusiastic harpists. The late Carmen Sylvia, Queen of Romania, devoted much of her time to it. Queen Elizabeth was also a harpist.
>
> The harp appeals to the romantic nature of women, and, indeed, there is no other instrument which so displays the charms of graceful feminity. Harp playing brings many opportunities for displaying the graceful movements of a pretty hand, arm and foot, to say nothing of the beautiful pose of the head, while the gold and artistic shape of the harp make an excellent foil for a beautiful gown. (Clark 4)

So much for carrying a harp to rouse the troops to battle. The feminization of the harp has resulted in its use in films dealing with themes of courtship, romance, gender, and sexual orientation, the latter also being a function of Hermes (Fig. 7.5).

The theme of the magic harp as being a female personality was explored in Disney's classic 1947 animated film *Mickey and the Beanstalk*. It's loosely based on the classic fairy tale of "Jack and the Beanstalk," recast with Disney characters; Mickey Mouse is Jack, and Donald Duck and Goofy come along to help. The story takes place in Happy Valley, which has become desolate ever since a giant named Willie made off with the magic harp, which lived in the castle on a hill at the center of the valley. Mickey, Donald, and Goofy climb up the beanstalk and discover the giant's castle. Inside, they discover the famous harp, which has been held hostage by the giant and forced to play at the master's beck and call (Figs. 7.6-7.8). Mickey and the gang rescue the harp and race

Screenshots from *Mickey and the Beanstalk*, Disney Studios, RKO Radio Pictures, 1947

Clockwise from top left:

7.6. The Magic Harp on the balcony of the giant's castle.

7.7. The Magic Harp singing to a bird. This character was later used as the model for the princess in the 1950 animated production of *Cinderella* by Disney Studios.

7.8. The harp's strings play magically.

7.9. Willie the Giant is lulled to sleep by the Magic Harp's music. When he is sound asleep, Mickey goes for the key to unlock the box where his buddies have been placed by the Giant.

7.10. The Magic Harp sings the directions for the key to Mickey as the Giant sleeps.

7.11. Mickey, Goofy, and Donald race down the Beanstalk with the Magic Harp chased by Willie the Giant.

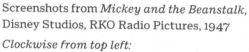

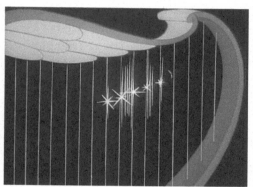

down the beanstalk with the giant in hot pursuit (Fig. 7.9). At the bottom they saw down the beanstalk and the giant falls to his reward from the sky. At the end of the tale, the harp is back in her castle and Happy Valley is restored to its former prosperity. The harp is a female angel that sings and plays. As with *The Aristocats*, her performance enchants the listeners. She charms not only the giant, Willie, to sleep but captures the attention of both Donald and Goofy (Figs. 7.10-7.11).

The metaphor of the female harp was taken to its most absurd realization in the 1934 Busby Berkeley musical *Fashions of 1934*, in the musical dream sequence with the "Hall of Human Harps." *Fashions*, directed by William Dieterle and starring William Powell and Bette Davis, is a comedy of deception and cheating that satirizes the superficiality of the fashion industry. Sherwood Nash (William Powell) is a swindler who bootlegs Paris fashions for sale at cut-rate prices. His assistant Lynn (Bette Davis) poses as an American interested in a dress. When they try to steal the latest Baroque designs hidden cameras capture them. Threat and counterthreat lead to the suggestion of putting on a legitimate fashion show. The plot also involves a deal marketing ostrich feathers, so the show is designed with them incorporated into the designs. The lavish production features the song "Spin a Little Web of Dreams." A review in *Variety* (1/23/34) commented, "The wow feather scene wherein Busby Berkeley combined a pageant of ostrich plumes to include a Hall of Human Harps, a Web of Dreams, and Venus and her Galley Slaves. Herein Berkeley again repeats the prismatic formations, dissolves, overhead shots and other of the now established school of BB cinematerps" (Pike and Martin 172).

The camera occupied the central position in Busby Berkeley's choreography. The popularity of his films caused Berkeley to turn increasingly toward film techniques to develop choreographic ideas. Along with editing, Berkeley manipulated time and space in his films and each of his dance productions were unique (Steinke 41).

The extravaganza features fan dancers who are mostly undressed. The scene opens with an overworked costume seamstress who falls asleep and has an elaborate dream. The scene cuts away to the "Hall of Human Harps" where some twenty stylized harps stand on pedestals while their crystal-beaded strings are stroked by ladies in flowing robes. The columns of the harps are statuesque, curvaceous females. According to Hal Erickson of *All Movie Guide*, *Fashions* is the picture in which these Berkeley beauties dressed as harps prompted the apocryphal admonition from a chorus girl's mother, "Mr. Berkeley, I didn't raise my daughter to be a human harp!" (Figs. 7.12-7.14).

"Spin a Little Web of Dreams" is such a female extravaganza that by the last movement featuring a bevy of galley slaves it begins to look more like some type of lesbian fantasy. "William Powell makes a good old rascal and Bette Davis all

Screenshots from *Fashions of 1934*, Warner Bros., 1934

Clockwise from top left:

7.12. Fan dancers opening the routine revealing the female human harps.

7.13. Ladies playing harps with female columns and beaded strings.

7.14. Close-up shot of the human harps.

dolled up in red lipstick and classy dresses, shows off a rare ability for humor, fitting right in to the film's light hearted tone," commented one viewer on the Internet Movie Database (http//us.imdb.com/Title?0025101).

In addition to the feminine form, the harp has also been used to showcase female performance in the cinema. Judy Garland played a small Irish harp in *In the Good Old Summertime* (1949). The ancestor of the 1998 hit *You've Got Mail* with Tom Hanks, *In the Good Old Summertime* is a remake of the 1940 version, *The Little Shop around the Corner*, and pairs Judy Garland up with Van Johnson. The film is best remembered for the final scene when Judy's daughter Liza Minnelli made her screen debut at two years old. In the story, Garland is a music store clerk corresponding with her unseen pen pal (Van Johnson) who also happens to be her boss. The owner of the music store, Otto Oberkugen (S. Z. Sakall), has purchased one hundred small Irish harps for resale but the shop staff thinks they are a bad investment. The instruments are diminutive with gold carved angel heads, reminiscent of the early Irish heraldry. Johnson particularly disagrees with Mr. Oberkugen's decision. The running joke throughout the story has Oberkugen lowering the initial price of the harps in the shop window as they refuse to sell.

Screenshots from *In the Good Old Summertime*, MGM, 1949

7.15. Judy Garland plays "Dreamland" on a small Irish harp in the music shop where she works with Van Johnson (middle) and S. Z. Sakall. As usual her hand positions are hardly worthy of a harpist and the soundtrack uses a larger pedal harp.

7.16. The harp is patterned after John Egan's Royal Portable Irish Harp with the female figurehead. Miss Garland might as well be playing a concert harp, as the soundtrack reveals.

In one scene, Judy Garland offers to play the music to "Dreamland," a song-sheet a customer wishes to purchase. Taking the small harp in hand, Garland amazingly plucks out the tune complete with glissandos and arpeggios (Fig. 7.15). Her hand positions manage to mimic a harpist but the concert harp on the soundtrack is too much to be believed. The customer is so entranced with Garland's performance that she also buys the first harp. (There's a Hermetic message here with music and commerce.) Garland originally began the song accompanied by Johnson at the piano, but she switches to the harp, and it makes a great prop for close-up shots during her song (Fig. 7.16).

A similar device is used in *The Wedding March*, Erich von Stroheim's 1928 extravaganza, which recreated the debauchery of the Habsburg society before the First World War. In *The Wedding March*, von Stroheim plays an impoverished prince (Nicki) who betrays his one true love and marries for money. Fay Wray (of *King Kong* fame) plays Mitzi, the pure and simple heroine who is a harpist at a Vienna beer garden with whom the prince has become enamored. In one scene, he secretly leaves the palace at night in order to court his beloved who is performing in the *haufgarten* playing the harp. Prince Nicki enters unseen and sits at the edge of the restaurant watching Mitzi pluck. She sees

Screenshots from *The Wedding March*, Paramount Pictures, 1928

Clockwise from top left:

7.17. Mitzi (Fay Wray of later *King Kong* fame) plays a harp in a beer garden in Vienna in 1914 when she catches the eye of Prince Nickolas von Wildeliebe-Rauffenburg, called Prince Nicki (played by Erich von Stroheim).

7.18. Prince Nicki sends admiring glances at Mitzi as she plays in the beer garden.

7.19. Close-up of Mitzi as she performs to the delight of Prince Nicki.

7.20. Seeing his admiration, Mitzi lifts her skirt while playing the harp.

7.21. Close up of a "well-turned ankle," as Melville Clark would have said.

him and begins to play a melody on the harp. As this was originally a silent film, the theatre organ supplied the musical background. In the reissued print by Paramount Home Video (1987), the organ used a special "harp" pipe-stop to mimic the harp in this scene. It sounds hokey but makes the character of the harp stand out. As a believable harpist, Fay Wray is a scream (Figs. 7.17-7.19). Her hand positions are almost as atrocious as the performers in *Fashions*. Of course, Prince Nicki is thoroughly captivated. Mitzi hefts up her skirts and displays her lame foot, which is in a cast due to an accident at the Corpus Christi parade where she first met the prince. One can only recall Melville Clark's comment that "harp playing brings many opportunities for displaying the graceful movements of a pretty hand, arm and foot." (Figs. 7.20-21).

Screenshots from *How the West Was Won*, MGM, 1962

7.22. Accompanied by a harp and violin, Debbie Reynolds performs an old folk song as a singer on a Sacramento riverboat.

7.23. Entranced by the sounds of the harp, Cleve (Gregory Peck) leaves his place at a gambling table and seeks out the source of the music.

7.24. Reunited, Cleve Van Valen (Gregory Peck) and Lillith Prescott (Debbie Reynolds) are married, and he seeks his fortune as a railroad tycoon in San Francisco.

A similar scene involving a harp in courtship occurs in MGM's 1962 release of *How the West Was Won*, which was filmed in Cinerama. Debbie Reynolds and Gregory Peck are paired up in this epic movie directed by John Ford. Peck plays a gambler (Cleve Van Valen) who had previously deserted Reynolds (Lilith Prescott) on a covered wagon trip from St. Louis to California. They meet again accidentally on a Sacramento riverboat where Reynolds is performing in the salon. Peck is amid a winning streak in a poker game when he hears the sound of a harp floating from the salon. He is distracted from the poker game and listens as the voice of Reynolds begins to sing "Home in the Meadow" to the

7.25. Jimmy Connors (Mickey Rooney) conducts the orchestra and chorus in the concluding musical number in *Strike Up the Band*, directed by Busby Berkeley, MGM/Warner Bros., 1940, screenshot

tune of "Greensleeves." Recognizing the voice and the tune, Peck snatches up his winnings and heads to the edge of the stage where he encounters Reynolds finishing her performance. They reunite and the flame of passion is rekindled. Peck offers his poker winnings and proposes on the spot. They marry and Peck becomes a millionaire railroad baron in San Francisco. Reynolds does not actually play the harp in this scene; she is the vocalist and is accompanied by a trio of harp, flute, and violin. It is the harp music. however, that alerts Peck at the gambling table. Hermes strikes again! (Figs. 7.22–7.24)

Mickey Rooney and Judy Garland were the ideal teenage couple of the forties. In *Strike Up the Band* (1940), directed by Busby Berkeley, they play high school teenagers with a big-band dream. Mickey is a gifted leader of a high school band hoping to compete in Paul Whiteman's nationwide radio contest. The plot revolves around Mickey and Judy as they struggle to make it happen. They cannot afford the fare but accidentally meet Paul Whiteman in person and he loans them the money after they convince him the band is good enough to compete. An unfortunate turn of events interrupts their plans, almost canceling the trip, but at the last minute they arrive at the contest and Mickey's band wins first place. An elaborate finale featuring Gershwin's title tune includes a sequence

Screenshots from *Strike Up the Band*, directed by Busby Berkeley, MGM, Warner Bros., 1940

7.26. Chorus girls surround a harpist in musical number.

7.27. Jimmy Connors (Mickey Rooney) and Mary Holden (Judy Garland) sing a duet accompanied by four identical pedal harps.

with Judy and Mickey singing in various sections of the orchestra. The camera features four blond harpists playing four identical gold concert harps. As they play, Mickey and Judy glide around them, ending up on a bench under a flowering tree in a romantic interlude. The harp shot is brief but powerful. Four identical blonds with four identical harps lead into a melody of romance (Figs. 7.25–7.27).

In *Dangerous Liaisons*, Keanu Reeves as the young harpsichord player manages to slip a handwritten note of affection to Uma Thurman by discreetly passing it through the harp strings during an arranged music lesson. As the underlying plot in *Dangerous Liaisons* involves lying and trickery, a written note passed between harp strings is the appropriate Hermetic touch (Fig. 7.28).

An interesting twist to the harp as a feminine symbol is using it to denote sexual orientation. In *Bedazzled*, the 2000 remake of Dudley Moore's 1967 film, Brendan Fraser plays a geeky loser (Elliot Richards) who sells his soul to the

7.28. A young suitor (Keanu Reeves) passes a love note through the strings to the harpist (Uma Thurman) in pre-French revolution Paris. *Dangerous Liaisons*, Warner Bros., 1988, screenshot

Devil for some wishes. However, nothing goes as planned and hilarity ensues. The story is a recycled version of Christopher Marlowe's "Dr. Faustus" and Edgar Allan Poe's "The Monkey's Paw." Elizabeth Hurley plays the female version of Satan in a revealing red dress who, in exchange for his immortal soul, grants Fraser seven wishes, which all center around him gaining the affection of a workmate he has fallen in love with.

The wishes are just flimsy excuses for Hurley to run Fraser through the wringer, and the film settles down into an extended series of skits as he lives out various fantasies, which go wrong in the usual Faustian/monkey's paw kind of way. We see Elliot as a Colombian drug lord, pro basketball player, sensitive New Age guy, and other personalities involved with his would-be lady love.

In one sketch, Elliot has made a wish to be a famous, witty literary celebrity. He instantly finds himself at a fashionable cocktail party in New York. Alison, his lady love (Frances O'Connor), is in attendance and falls under Elliot's charms. He then invites her home, and we see them arriving in his stylish Upper East Side apartment. Looking around, she exclaims: "O this is so perfect! Everything I see screams Elliot Richards!" Elliot (Fraser) replies, "Actually, all the screaming actually takes place in the . . . bedroom," sweeping Alison off her feet and carrying her into the bedroom (Fig. 7.29).

In the following shot as they enter the bedroom, there is a concert harp with music stand in the background (Figs. 7.30–7.31). Elliot stands, holding Alison, looking into her eyes when suddenly there is a scratching sound and the sound of flying sheets and a voice screaming, *"What the hell is going on, Mary?"* Fraser looks to see a man in silk pajamas climbing out of the bed. "Who are you?" Fraser replies, confused. "Don't play games with me, Mr. Richards, I'm in no mood! I've been out of my mind all night." Elliot looks at the man, then at Alison, and it hits him. "Oh my god! I'm not *gay*!" "Oh yeah, if you're not gay then I'm Tony Danza!" replies his partner. "I'm not gay!" he says to Alison. "Let me prove it to you. Kiss me!" he says to her. They embrace in a passionate kiss. "You're

Screenshots from *Bedazzled*, Regency Enterprises, Twentieth Century Fox, 2000

7.29. Elliot Richards (Brendan Fraser) as a rich and famous writer in one fantasy sequence of *Bedazzled* finally whisks his love interest Alison (Frances O'Connor) into his bedroom "where most of the screaming happens."

7.30. Much to his surprise, Elliot is greeted by a male lover in this fantasy, who demands to know where he has been all night and who is with him. Notice the pedal harp prominently placed in the bedroom. Why would a harp be in a bedroom?

7.31. Elliot realizes he has been tricked again by the Devil (Elizabeth Hurley).

right. I *am* gay," he says as he pulls away from Alison. "Well, I guess I had better say good night," she says abruptly. "Okay, good night," he replies hastily.

She exits and the man in the bed goes on ranting, "You're drunk. Just like that time at Fire Island when you drank all those brandy Alexanders and sang 'Evergreen' running up and down the beach in those speedos!" Fraser screams, and he is taken from the scene and back to the presence of the Devil (Hurley).

Throughout this scene a harp stands in the background of the bedroom. So what's the connection? We know that the harp has been feminized and Hermes is the trickster. In this scene the harp serves as a visual cue in the stereotypical fashion as a gay symbol. A large statue of Michelangelo's *David* might have made a similar statement, but it would not have had the same effect.

As the trickster, Hermes might be considered the patron of gay culture. He not only inspires quick wit and verbal agility but also spitefulness, gossip, stealth, and guile. In addition, he is the boundary-crosser and psychopomp who travels between worlds. He is also the Devil in the Tarot, which symbolizes bondage to superficial realities. All of this could be applied to homosexuality, although most gay people are unaware of its significance. In bringing up the subject of homosexuality, I am not implying that the harp is a gay instrument or that all harpists are gay but that the archetypal image of Hermes as inventor of the lyre and as trickster lends itself to the gay sensitivity.[1]

Literature in gay psychology mentions the significance of the *berdache*, "a term used by early French explorers to describe a certain figure who occupied a certain role in many of the Native American tribes they came across, a role unknown or persecuted in Western European societies: that of an anatomical male who dressed as a woman and assumed an important position of great tribal importance" (Hopcke 174).[2]

> The berdache clearly forms a third sex in native societies, a gender-sex role status sometimes referred to as mixed-gender by anthropologists. The role of the berdache in native cultures is largely spiritual. They carry the function of the Self for the tribe and function as spiritual leaders: presiding at ritual events, granting spiritual power names to children, healing, prophesying, and generally performing the role of shaman in the tribe. Because of this clearly understood connection to the divine, the berdaches are honored members of the tribes and tend to represent the best and the brightest of the society in terms of wealth, social prestige, and tribal power (Hopcke 176).

The shaman or berdache has always been androgynous. Hopcke writes that the concept of the berdache gives a social and psychological form to an essential and archetypal gay experience, that of bringing the opposites of male and female experience together through living an acknowledged connection to one's homosexuality as a spiritual reality (Hopcke 181).

Hopcke also points out a Hermetic connection:

> These androgynous images of miraculous male pregnancies, physical contact with acquaintances who are simultaneously male and female, cross dressing, and division into male-female couples all point out how Hermes, messenger of the gods, and Aphrodite, the goddess of love and physical connection, unite into the sometimes monstrous, sometimes unifying image of the gay male Hermaphrodite. The pattern of androgyny seen in the North American berdache tradition has archetypal roots, and Jung's ideas on the nature and function of the Hermaphrodite are an important tool in understanding many characteristics of these figures: their sacredness, their mediatory functions, their usefulness to the continuation of society and the family, their shamanistic endowment, and their ability to reconcile the opposites of male and female for themselves and others. This pattern of androgyny is one archetypal pattern that, alongside the feminine and masculine patterns, appears in the lives of contemporary gay men. (Hopcke 185)

The trickster element involves a perception of reality that distinguishes the homosexual from the heterosexual. Again, as Robert Hopcke writes in his essay, "The Union of the Sames," in *Gay Soul*:

> Because enacting homosexual sexuality is often forbidden or discouraged, the one thing that accounts for a lot of gay men's unconsciousness is the conflict around their sexuality—either they don't enact it and continue to repress it or they act it out all over the place in an unreflective kind of way. Gay culture in general supports a very literalistic way of thinking about sexuality, as opposed to a more symbolic or deeper way. In a certain sense what happens, then, is that gay men don't fully appreciate the power of sexual action. Being gay is very different from a heterosexual's experience, in which everything they see, hear, and have been told confirms their own experience. Whereas for gay men and lesbians, their experience is at odds with what they're told. And so you have this sense—like in *The Wizard of Oz* myth—that everything isn't really what it seems. That's gay people's gift. Gay people are perceived as having more freedom. In fact, perhaps we do, since we're free from this myth. (Hopcke 219)

The sense that everything isn't really what it seems is also the symbolism behind the tarot card depicting the Devil: the illusion of bondage to superficial realities. It is the basis of gay humor and entertainment such as female impersonation drag shows. No harpist was straighter than Harpo Marx. He saw the power of humor in the instrument and was one of the first to exploit that on screen. Our next chapter will consider the harp in comedy and fantasy in film.

COMEDY AND FANTASY

*If you've ever seen a Marx Brothers picture, you know the
difference between him and me. When he sits down to play
the harp, it's Me. Whenever I touched the strings of the harp,
I stopped being an actor.*

—Harpo Marx

The harp is not only a sexy instrument, but it is a visual instrument as well. Its basic form has changed little in a thousand years, and the idea of so many strings available to touch has given rise to numerous humorous jokes and opportunities for slapstick humor. Probably the most famous use of the instrument in comedy was in the Marx Brothers movies, although the harp has been featured in several other films, including animated films.

Harpo Marx originally took up the harp to differentiate himself from his brother Chico, who already played the piano in the budding vaudeville act. Harpo's mother, Minnie, who served as the act's manager, bought one and had it shipped to him while they were on the road in Aurora, Illinois. Harpo writes in his autobiography, *Harpo Speaks*, that the harp was in the act after only two weeks, even though Harpo couldn't read a note of music:

> I found out that the price of my harp was forty-five dollars (ten bucks of Minnie's money down and one buck of my money per week). This gave me new respect for the instrument. Groucho got new respect for it, too. Groucho I could now drown out—his voice, his guitar or his mandolin— any time I wanted to, with a lusty swipe on the harp strings.
>
> The presence of the harp (the harp alone, and not the harpist) had raised our average monthly income by five dollars. (Marx 125)

Harpo was as initially self-taught on the harp, and he became so accomplished that the only formal harp instructor he had, a harpist with the Metropolitan Opera Company, charged Harpo twenty dollars for a lesson and ended up learning all of Harpo's techniques for himself.

The nearest I've had to a regular teacher has been a lady named Mildred Dilling. I first met her in a music store where she was trying out a new harp. She was playing a piece called "The Music Box." I introduced myself and confessed that I couldn't read notes, and asked her if she would please teach me to play "The Music Box." She was delighted to. We soon became good friends. It was she who introduced me to the world of Bach and Mozart, Debussy and Ravel.

Like all others, Miss Dilling never tried to change my screwball technique. But she was glad to help me in any other way. Many a time I've telephoned her (sometimes from across the country, waking her up in the middle of the night) when I've gotten stuck on a tricky chord. Night or day, she wouldn't fail me. She'd hitch her harp close to the phone in her studio and play the chord over and over until I got it, at the other end of the wire. What you might call an Extension Course. (Marx 185)

The Marx Brothers developed their unique slapstick and ensemble word-play style on the vaudeville stage, then adapted to the movies. They specialized in spoofing high society with their antics and skirt-chasing (Fig. 8.1). Their success was due in large part to the interest of Irving Thalberg at MGM who developed a formula in Marx Brothers films that resulted in the wild popularity of films like *A Night at the Opera* and *A Day at the Races*. The film plots usually included musical interludes by Chico, Groucho, or Harpo. "Thalberg's formula was that if there must be musical scenes and romance, they are tolerable if strategically placed. One of the key stratagems of Thalberg's formula is the 'low point,' that moment at which all seems dark for the brothers, their plans dashed, their hopes blank, the prospects of the romantic couple equally bare. The so-called logic behind this is to allow the brothers to rise to even greater heights by comparison. So these low points invariably fall as the movie rounds the backstretch before heading into its triumphant finale" (Zimmerman 137).

In one instance, Harpo uses the harp as a bow, shooting arrows from a stretched string. Salvador Dali, an avid fan of the Marx Brothers, actually painted a portrait of Harpo at a harp that Dali created, which was strung with barbed wire and had knives and forks glued all over it.[1] Harpo had developed his own playing style and frequently played with getting his fingers caught in the strings. However, when Harpo actually sat down to play, his demeanor changed, and he became a different person while actually performing. One of the best illustrations of this change occurs in the scene in *A Day at the Races*, which was described in Chapter I. Harpo picks up the harp from within the destroyed piano and launches into a solo that transforms the scene briefly before resuming its madcap pace.

In the early days, the audience had confused his voice with brothers Zeppo and Chico, so Harpo decided he would no longer speak in public and used a

8.2. Harpo Marx in another world playing the harp

8.1. The three Marx Brothers peering out through Harpo's harp. Groucho (left), Harpo (center), and Chico (right)

8.3. Harpo's expression changes completely when he is engaged with his harp

variety of horns, bells, and whistles to communicate. The harp became Harpo's voice after he adapted the mime persona. Ironically, the lord of speech and the trickster thus communicates through Harpo's instrument and Groucho's double-talk (Figs. 8.2–8.3)

There is also a funny scene involving the harp in a nonmusical way. In Disney's *The Absent-Minded Professor* (1961), Fred MacMurray (Professor Ned Brainard) has invented a mysterious substance, "flubber," which makes things fly. He and his fiancé Nancy Olsen (Betsy Carlisle) are sneaking into a prop room in an attempt to elude some thugs who are involved with an attempt to steal MacMurray's invention—the flying flubber. MacMurray steals into the room but knocks over a harp. In attempting to catch it, he accidentally puts his foot directly through the strings. The humorous situation develops as he and his girlfriend attempt to extricate his foot from between the strings without making any noise. Naturally, a string pings and the guys outside hear it. "Say, did you hear what I just did?" one thug asks the other one. "Sounds like . . . like . . . like a *harp*?" MacMurray struggles with his foot. Another note pings. "See . . . there it goes again!" The second thug replies, "Remember Foxy McKenna? Instead of

Screenshots from *The Absent-Minded Professor,* Walt Disney Productions, 1961

8.4. In *The Absent-Minded Professor,* Fred MacMurray (Professor Ned Brainard) accidentally stumbles when sneaking into a warehouse looking for his stolen car and accidentally steps through the strings of a harp.

8.5. Professor Brainard (Mac-Murray) and his girlfriend, Betsy Carlisle (Nancy Olsen), attempt to free Brainard's entangled foot without making a sound.

8.6. Struggling to free his foot, Brainard and Carlisle elude the warehouse guards.

harp noises, he kept hearing bird calls!" MacMurray struggles again. Plunk! The thug shakes his head. He can't tell if he is hallucinating or not (Figs. 8.4-8.6).

In Mel Brooks film *High Anxiety* (1981), there's a humorous scene when Brooks is being pursued on the highway and has a sudden panic attack. Suddenly there's an orchestral chord denoting anxiety and as it unfolds, a bus painted with a sign saying "Los Angeles Symphony" passes Brooks. On the bus are members of the orchestra playing the music on the soundtrack as they pass by with the most conspicuous instrument being the harpist playing a harp between the seats (Figs. 8.7-8.8).

The concept of the soundtrack becoming part of the visual humor is better exemplified in a scene from the 1971 Woody Allen comedy film *Bananas.* Allen as the central character plays a bumbling New Yorker who, after being dumped by his activist girlfriend, travels to a tiny Latin American nation and becomes involved in its latest rebellion. In one scene he hears a knock at the door of his

Screenshots from *High Anxiety*, Twentieth Century Fox, 1977

8.7–8.8. Mel Brooks as Dr. Richard Harpo Thorndyke, a famous psychiatrist, is hired to run the Psycho-Neurotic Institute for the Very Very Nervous. In this parody of Alfred Hitchcock films Brooks has a moment of sudden panic (underscored by a harp glissando in the soundtrack). Just as he is experiencing this emotion, a bus passes him carrying the entire LA Symphony Orchestra playing the soundtrack. Prominent is a harpist playing the instrument backwards between the seats of the bus.

Screenshots from *Bananas*, United Artists, 1971

8.9. Hearing the glissando of a harp, Fielding Mellish (Woody Allen) has a moment of revelation following a formal invitation to have dinner with the President.

8.10. Mellish (Woody Allen) discovers the source of the glissandos—a male harpist sitting in his hotel room closet.

hotel room. When he answers the door, he is met by an official messenger who delivers a personal invitation to dine at the palace with the country's president. After the messenger leaves, Allen closes the door and begins contemplating the significance of this information. Suddenly, while lost in contemplation, there is heard a dramatic glissando from a harp. Allen goes over to the closet doors and opens them, revealing a guy sitting in the closet making the glissandos. He apologizes to Allen for disturbing him as the closet was the only private place he

Screenshots from *Unfaithfully Yours,* Twentieth Century Fox, 1948

8.11. As the orchestra rehearses a movement,
the camera pans across the stage to reveal two
harpists waiting for their segment. One is knit-
ting and the other is polishing her fingernails.

8.12. Harpists waiting for their cues.

8.13. Harpist inspecting her nails. Harpists have
to have short nails to properly pluck the strings.

could find to practice. A great sight gag and the astute harpist will notice that
the prop harp is only half strung! (Figs. 8.9-8.10).

Several comedy films exploit the orchestral setting. In *Unfaithfully Yours*
(1948), directed by Preston Sturges, there is a shot of a symphony orchestra
playing a movement and the camera pans around the string section to the harp
section, revealing two harps with the two respective harpists relaxing and fil-
ing their nails—a marvelous jab at the notion that harpists have lots of time

between their parts. This is an effective joke as the harp has often been perceived as a limited instrument due to its earlier lack of chromaticism and limited repertoire (Figs. 8.11–8.13).

Another scene occurs in the French comedy *The Tall Blond Man with One Black Shoe* (*Le grand blonde avec une chaussure noire*) (1973). The plot concerns an innocent musician (Pierre Richard) caught in a web of counterintelligence surveillance between two competing government agencies. He is a violinist with a symphony orchestra and his girlfriend is the harpist. In one tense scene during a concert filled with agents and counteragents, Richard is supposed to be playing the lead violin solo. Unnerved, he bumbles his way through the passage. At one point the violin bow slips from his hand landing on the floor. The orchestra is silent as he scrambles across several other violinists to retrieve his bow. Meanwhile, the harp keeps playing an impromptu chord to cover for him. The conductor, who has been trying to ignore the situation, finally shouts "STOP IT!" to the harpist (Figs. 8.14–8.16).

Screenshots from *The Tall Blond Man with One Black Shoe*, Gaumont, 1972

Clockwise from top left:

8.14. François Perrin (Pierre Richard) is an incompetent violinist who has lost his bow during a concert and jumps up to find it during a musical interlude.

8.15. While Francois is searching for his violin bow, his harpist girlfriend provides an impromptu cadenza on the harp as a distraction.

8.16. "Stop it!" the conductor yells to the harpist when he realizes she is playing to cover the violinist.

Screenshots from *Bugsy Malone*, Paramount, 1976

8.17. *"Next!"* the director calls for the next act on the audition stage. A stagehand drags a pedal harp from the wings followed by a young performer in a long gown.

8.18. *"Next! Next!"* the director dismisses the harp without even considering it.

The harp has also been used in animated cartoons. Bugs Bunny played it and had his head squeezed between the strings in one *Looney Tunes* sequence. In a *Tiny Toon Adventures* sequence, Buster Bunny becomes a ghost and haunts his assassin by playing a harp. The scene from this example would also fit nicely into Chapter IV, "The Heavenly Instrument."

In a final example, the harp mystique is panned in *Bugsy Malone* (1976), a 1930s gangster and musical spoof with all the characters played by children. Instead of real bullets, they use "splat guns" that cover the victim in cream or custard pies. The story tells of the rise of "Bugsy Malone" and the battle for power between "Fat Sam" and "Dandy Dan." The most identifiable star is Jodie Foster, who was thirteen when the film was made.

In a Broadway variety show auditioning scene, the director and his assistant (both children made up as adults) are sitting in an empty theater previewing a lineup of talent acts for an upcoming production. First comes a comedy routine. After a few lines, the director shouts dismissively, "Next!" Then there is a vocal number, which is also rejected after a few bars, "Not that old chestnut again! . . . Next!" Then a ventriloquist (played by Jodie Foster) offers a few lines. "Next!" Then a magician pulls a rabbit out of a hat. "Next!" Finally, the stagehands come pulling a gold concert harp followed by a young lady in a long flowing dress, which prompts the director without hesitation to shout, "Next! . . . Next! Next!" and the film cuts to the next scene. The image said it all; the harpist didn't play a note (Figs. 8.17–8.18).

CIVILIZATION AND CULTURE

Poets are the unacknowledged legislators of the world.
—Percy Bysshe Shelley

As we have seen in this study, the harp has been most often associated with the immaterial world and etheric themes. However, it was also pointed out that because of its divine associations, the instrument has been the companion of royalty and the upper strata of society since ancient times. The earliest examples of royal lyres excavated at the Royal Cemetery at Ur (c. 2600–2350 BC) were highly decorated with gold leaf and precious gems (Fig. 9.1). Musical instruments are signs of a developed civilization, which has achieved a level of stability in which time and resources can be devoted to the higher arts such as music and painting. So, the harp has become a symbol of material culture as well.

9.1. Silver lyre with inlaid front (restored) from "The Great Death Pit" at Ur, c. 2500 BC, The British Museum, postcard

Screenshots from *Gone with the Wind*, Selznick International Pictures, MGM, 1939

9.2. Scarlett O'Hara (Vivien Leigh) leaves the makeshift hospital in Atlanta only to be confronted by the fleeing residents as Sherman's troops approach Atlanta. Notice the uncovered gold pedal harp in the wagon at the bottom of the frame.

9.3. Close-up shot as the wagonload of domestic treasures rounds the corner in Atlanta before the approaching Union Army.

Probably the most famous film shot depicting this idea occurs in MGM's 1939 classic *Gone With the Wind*. In Margaret Mitchell's story of the Old South, the Civil War and Reconstruction serve as the background to the famous love story between Scarlett O'Hara and Rhett Butler. Scarlett O'Hara (Vivien Leigh), newly widowed, goes to Atlanta to stay with her Aunt Pittypat. She is working as a nurse in the Confederate hospital during the siege of Atlanta and in one famous scene, Scarlett leaves the hospital to discover panic in the streets of Atlanta. Sherman is closing in on the city and the residents are fleeing. The camera pans from Scarlett out to the confusion in the street. Wagons loaded with refugees rush past. Suddenly a loaded wagon races by with a gold harp pitched precariously in the load (Figs. 9.2-9.3). The shot follows the wagon as it joins hundreds of other wagons in the flight. Any harpist would tell you that nobody would transport a harp without either a cover or a harp trunk but the image here is of panic and the salvage of a way of life. The exposed harp says it all—the last shred of civilization (as Southerners would know it) is racing to escape the conflagration ... *gone with the wind.*[1]

Screenshots from *Empire of the Sun*, Amblin Entertainment, Warner Bros., 1987

Clockwise from top left:

9.4. A chauffeur polishes the family Packard with its swan hood ornament while Jim (Christian Bale) is in choir practice rehearsal.

9.5. Close-up of the Packard's swan hood ornament.

9.6. Shot of the football stadium near Nantao, where many of the Shanghai inhabitants' possessions have been stored by the Japanese.

In Steven Spielberg's *Empire of the Sun* (1987), there is a similar visual statement. *Empire of the Sun* is based on J. G. Ballard's autobiographical novel and tells the story of an English boy, James Graham, whose privileged life is upturned by the Japanese invasion of Shanghai in December 1941. Separated from his parents, he is eventually captured and taken to the Soo Chow confinement camp, next to a captured Chinese airfield. Amid the sickness and food shortages in the camp, Jim attempts to reconstruct his former life, all while bringing spirit and dignity to those around him (Hansen).

At the beginning of the story, we see that the boy's parents are wealthy British citizens who enjoy a life of great luxury in Shanghai, a life in which limousines hurry them through the crowded streets to business meetings and parties and they hardly need notice the ordinary people in those streets. The Chinese are almost invisible until the war breaks out and the boy's whole world is shattered.

In an early scene, the camera focuses on the family car, a huge British model with a silver swan mounted on the hood (Figs. 9.4-9.5). When the Japanese seize Shanghai, they loot the British residential neighborhood where James (Christian Bale) and his family lived in regal comfort. All of the furnishings and accessories are removed from the homes and are deposited in the soccer stadium outside of town (Fig. 9.6). Jim's accidental separation from his parents occurs when they lose him in a crowd of five thousand Chinese fleeing Shanghai. He does not

Screenshots from *Empire of the Sun*, Amblin Entertainment, Warner Bros., 1987

Clockwise from top:

9.7. Wide-angle shot of interior of the stadium showing plundered items from the British residents of Shanghai.

9.8. Close-up of Jim as he spots his family Packard. Notice the pedal harp in the background.

9.9-9.10. Jim approaches the family Packard focusing on the swan hood ornament.

see them until four years later at the end of the war. Jim is eventually captured by the Japanese and placed in a detention camp for British prisoners, where he learns to survive on his wits and his love of airplanes regardless of politics.

In a climactic scene near the end of the story, the Japanese, sensing defeat, march the British prisoners from their destroyed camp at a captured Chinese airbase to the soccer stadium. There the prisoners discover a collection of items that the Japanese had removed from their homes at the beginning of the war.

Exhausted, Jim wanders in to see the family car with the swan hood ornament. As the camera focuses in on the car, we see in the background a variety of stolen accessories and furnishings: crystal chandeliers, statuary, a piano, and standing prominently just to left of center—a harp! (Figs. 9.7–9.10).

All of the trappings of British culture in Shanghai were deposited here. Exhausted, Jim spends the night surrounded by these symbols of the past. Typical of Spielberg, we are given detailed close-ups of statues and clinking chandelier crystals. Jim awakens in the early morning to witness the flash of the atomic bomb racing across the sky from the east, which he thinks is the soul of Mrs. Victor (Miranda Richardson), who has died during the night in Jim's arms. Only later when we hear a radio announcement of the bombing of Hiroshima do we realize that the flash was from the bomb and not Mrs. Victor's soul flying heavenward. While the swan hood ornament was the film's primary symbol for Jim's status in a changing world, the harp is a cinematic abbreviation for culture.

In Steven Spielberg's *Amistad* (1997), the harp serves as a political symbol. The film deals with an accurate historical story of the 1839 revolt by Africans on the slave ship *Amistad* and their capture and trial in New Haven, Connecticut. Much of the story involves courtroom drama featuring the slave Cinque (Dijmon Hounsou), who led the revolt. Film reviewer Dennis Schwartz writes, "The relevance and devastating emotions of the slaves were intelligently presented" (Schwartz).

The thrust of the plot revolves around two courtroom trials to determine the fate of the fifty-three Africans captured off the coast following their shipboard revolt. The touchy question is whether these people were "legal" slaves born in Cuba or whether they were actually newly captured Africans en route from Africa to the Americas via Havana? It is a loaded question, as slavery had been outlawed both in Britain and parts of the United States. Spielberg casts President Martin Van Buren (Nigel Hawthorne) as guilty of kowtowing to Southern slaveholding interests. It's an election year and Van Buren is reminded of the mounting pressure regarding state sovereignty over slavery matters by John C. Calhoun. Van Buren wishes the matter to go away. In fact, he attempts to fix the first court case, which, if decided as he wished, would condemn the fifty-three Africans imprisoned in New Haven to execution in Cuba or Spain. Van Buren makes no outward stand, to the frustration of his advisors. He is seen as a do-nothing president—"fiddling while Rome burns."

In the meantime, former president John Quincy Adams, played by Anthony Hopkins with an American accent, is brought in to argue the case before the Supreme Court and makes the final moral point. If these men are not set free, the Civil War might as well begin now. He then proceeds to rip up a piece of paper to symbolize the death of the Declaration of Independence. "Spielberg is the master of the visual story, and here he is in top form. The carnage and cruelty aboard the slave ship are shockingly and revealingly shot, giving one enough of an idea what the slave had to endure. That gives the film the force and importance that is needed for it to make its moral point" (Schwartz 3) (Figs. 9.11–9.13).

In the White House scenes with incumbent president Van Buren, there is a

Screenshots from *Amistad*, HBO
Pictures, DreamWorks Pictures,
1997

9.11. A ship of the Royal Marines
fires cannons at the Lomboko slave
fortress in Sierra Leone.

9.12-9.13. Captain Fitzgerald orders
the Marines to destroy the Lomboko
fortress.

9.14-9.15. Simultaneous with the destruction of the Lomboko Fortress in Sierra
Leone, President Van Buren, facing reelection, tunes his harp in the White House.
Nero fiddles while Rome burns, and Van Buren loses the election to Harrison.

gold harp standing in the room where his advisors meet and discuss the impotency of the president. At the conclusion of the story, after Cinque and his fellow prisoners have been freed and returned to Africa, a British warship destroys the illegal slave fortress in the West Indies, from which the *Amistad* had sailed with its slave cargo. Spielberg cuts between the shots of the exploding fortress to shots of President Van Buren in the White House tuning the harp with a small tinkling bell (Figs. 9.14-9.15). It's as if Nero is tuning his lyre as Rome burns. The ugly political situation regarding slavery has been avoided only to return in the future in 1861. An additional political meaning could refer to the similar Irish situation and the earlier remark that "it cost more to keep the damned thing in tune than it was worth."

Peter Sellers and Ringo Starr perform a harp-and-recorder duet in *The Magic Christian*, the cynical 1969 film written by Terry Southern that says that anything can be bought and that everyone has their price. Peter Sellers stars as the obscenely wealthy Sir Guy Grand, who manages to seem almost childlike as he spreads his bounty of cynicism throughout London. He picks up a homeless man (Ringo Starr) and adopts him as his son and then goes about a series of escapades that slams the stuffed shirts of upper-class London society. *The Magic Christian* is a disjointed work of social satire with psychedelic sixties references. The title refers to a bogus cruise ship that Sellers creates. He then touts the inaugural voyage as the social event of the season.

In one scene, Peter Sellers is seated at a harp playing a classical piece with Ringo in the living room of Sellers's mansion (Figs. 9.16-9.17). They are conversing about writing a pornographic novel with blank spaces so the reader can insert his own words. The actual scene is minor to the plot; however, it depicts Sellers as a sensitive and artistic individual in spite of his material wealth. During their playing there is a montage of sixties antiwar riots and street fights. A viewer review on the *Internet Movie Database* commented, "Film aficionados will appreciate the many old-line British actors who contributed supporting or cameo roles (Spike Milligan, Lawrence Harvey, Richard Attenborough, John Le Mesurier, Wilfrid Hyde-White, Christopher Lee, and others less known outside the UK) as well as John Cleese and Graham Chapman of early Monty Python fame."

The culminating example of the harp as a cultural icon concerns Woody Allen's film *Small Time Crooks* (2000). In this Manhattan-based story, Allen plays an ex-con dishwasher with Tracey Ullman as Frances "Frenchy" Fox, his stripper-turned-manicurist wife. Allen hatches a scheme to rob a bank from a next-door pizza shop by tunneling from beneath the pizza shop into the bank. He enlists Ullman to front the shop, only she can't bake pizza but knows how to bake cookies. So, they open a cookie shop and Allen and his nitwit buddies attempt an idiotic scheme to tunnel into the bank. However, the crime goes bust while Frenchy's cookie business takes off wildly. It is such a big hit that she's

Screenshots from *The Magic
Christian*, Commonwealth United
Corporation, 1969,

9.16. Ringo Starr (Young Man
Grand) on recorder and Peter
Sellers (Sir Guy Grand) at the harp.

9.17. The two men play a duet in
the living room of Sir Guy Grand's
mansion.

catapulted into stardom as a cookie mogul. The business is franchised and run
by Ray (Allen) and his two-bit crooks. The rest of the movie revolves around
Frenchy's attempts to get class and Ray's efforts to shun it like the plague
(Rhodes review).

"With their new found wealth they turn their lavish, new Manhattan apartment into a garish imitation of a bad bordello with more gold than Fort Knox,"
writes Steve Rhodes. Their home, as Frenchy brags, has a rug with fiber optics
that light up in order to create the right ambience. Their outlandish outfits
match the decor perfectly.

In the first scene after they become rich, we are led into the living room by
the camera, which focuses on an elaborate gold concert harp standing in the
center of the room. Frenchy, dressed in a pink bathrobe with her hair in rollers,
is fussing around directing the placement of the objets d'art. "You know," she
says to the servants, "I think it's better in the first place I had it. Darling, could
you put the doll over there by the ceramic zebra? And Stevens, could you get
that piece Mr. Winkler hates and put it out by the fireplace?" Then the chef

Screenshots from *Small Time Crooks*, Sweetland Films, DreamWorks, 2000

9.18. A gold harp graces the upper living room of Frances "Frenchy" Fox-Winkler (Tracy Ullman) who is busily decorating her new townhouse.

9.19. *"What's that thing doing there?"* Ray (Woody Allen) points toward the gold harp in the living room.

9.20. *"It's a harp, Ray. You've got no flair, Ray,"* responds Frenchy. Ray retorts, *"Don't tell me I've got no flair! Nobody plays the harp. Who plays it? What's it doing in the middle of the living room?"* he asks. *"I like the visual sweep!"* she responds.

comes out of the kitchen, and they discuss the evening's menu including truffles and escargot ("snails" as Frenchy calls them). She wants fingerbowls because "you can never tell when somebody needs to wash their fingers."

Meanwhile, Ray (Allen) returns to the apartment from an appointment. He takes one look around and remarks, "Did you rearrange this place again?" "All right, all right. Hold your water!" she responds. "Don't tell me to hold my water! Every time I come home to this place, it's like walking into a strange house." He walks into the living room and looks at the harp. "What's this thing here?"

gesturing toward the harp. "Didn't I tell you to get rid of this thing?" "It's a harp. You've got no flair, Ray," she replies.

"Don't tell me I've got no flair! Nobody plays the harp. Who plays it? What's it doing in the middle of the living room?" he asks in classic Allen anxious style. "I like the *visual sweep*!" she says. Looking worried, he says, "You know, I don't know what's gotten into your head. You've gotten so hoity-toity all of a sudden!" "Hey! It's my cookies that pays for all this so turn it off!" she replies (Figs. 9.18-9.20).

Looking around, he says, "What's for dinner? Don't tell me it's gonna be little sparrows on a bed of lettuce again. Cause I don't care if I ever had anything on a bed of lettuce anymore." "They're pheasants and you ate them last week," she says. "Yeah, and I got a BB in my mouth. Remember, I almost choked on a BB?"

Later that evening, they host a dinner party in an attempt to meet people with social connections. As the guests arrive, Frenchy guides them around the foyer.

"Did you decorate this place yourself, Frances?" one guest asks. "Yes, they say I have a flair for decorating!" Frenchy gushes. A gentleman looks at the harp and remarks, "Do you play the harp, Frances?" "No, no. It's a *visual*, honey. The *sweep*! It kills me."

So, at last, the harp has come from being the "heavenly instrument" to a *visual*, a design element, the ultimate statement of culture and refinement. It extends an archetypal power even to those who are unconscious of its significance or its musical qualities.

In concluding this chapter on the image of the harp and civilization, I am reminded of Carl Jung's comments in *The Archetypes and the Collective Unconsciousness*:

> Like personalities, these archetypes are true and genuine symbols that cannot be exhaustively interpreted, either as signs or as allegories. They are genuine symbols precisely because they are ambiguous, full of half-glimpsed meanings, and in the last resort inexhaustible. (Jung 38)

CONCLUSION

While I was undertaking this study on the archetypal nature of the harp, worldwide audiences were watching the release of what was, at the time, the most highly anticipated and promoted film of the twenty-first century: *Harry Potter and the Sorcerer's Stone*. The film adaptation follows the original novel by J. K. Rowling quite closely with a few minor alterations.

In the story, Harry and his classmates Hermione and Ron are seeking the Sorcerer's Stone, which they believe to be hidden in a secret chamber in the depths of Hogwarts, their school of wizardry and witchcraft. The chamber is guarded by a giant three-headed dog named Fluffy. When Harry and his companions realize the stone is in danger of falling into the wrong hands, they rush to the chamber and discover that Fluffy has been magically put to sleep, and music flows from the room. In the corner stands a gold harp playing itself as if by invisible hands. "Look!" cries Ron, "Fluffy's asleep! Snape has cast a spell on

C.1. Harry (Daniel Radcliffe), Hermione Granger (Emma Watson), and Ron Weasley (Rupert Grint) struggle to open the trapdoor to the vault without waking the three-headed guard dog while the harp lulls him to sleep. *Harry Potter and the Sorcerer's Stone*, Warner Bros., 2001, screenshot

the harp and the music has put him to sleep!" The harp plays on and we can see the strings vibrating. They pass by the dog and struggle to open the trapdoor in the floor (Fig. C.1). Unnoticed, the harp stops, and as the music fades, Fluffy begins to awaken. Suddenly he is up with all three heads growling fiercely. Ron and Harry manage to get down before Fluffy blocks them and they proceed to the next chamber and the exciting conclusion of the plot.

Two points about this scene demonstrate my thesis. First, there is the scene itself. In the book, Hermione plays a flute or whistle to distract the dog, but in the film version a harp is used. Here is the visual statement of the archetypal power of the harp, and here are once again Hermes and Orpheus charming the beast. Like the stories of "Jack and the Beanstalk" and "David and Goliath," music has charmed the forces of danger and soothed them into submission. The directors of the film purposely chose a harp because they were working on a mythic story. No other musical instrument can quite make this statement as effectively. The harp is playing magically because of a spell cast on it. We are in the presence of the trickster. The characters experience boundary-crossing when they pass Fluffy and enter the struggle of good vs. evil, which is Harry's ultimate mission.

Secondly, *Harry Potter and the Sorcerer's Stone* played to a worldwide audience as the first film marketed on a global scale. As a result of the merger of Warner-Time-AOL, etc., Harry Potter was being exploited in every conceivable media format throughout the world at the same time. Thus, in the most popular film of 2001, we are again gathered in "Plato's cave" communing with archetypal themes of good and evil and we cross the boundary of imagination with Harry into the secret chamber of destiny with the aid of Hermes's instrument.

Two films that I might add to this study are Greta Gerwig's *Little Women* (2019) and Stanley Doren's *Once More, with Feeling* (1960) with Yul Brynner and Kay Kendall. In *Little Women*, one of the girls, Beth March (Eliza Scanlen), has a talent for piano and is invited to her wealthy neighbor's home to play the piano that belonged to his deceased daughter. In the scene, Beth walks into a grand salon where she approaches a pianoforte and just beyond stands a beautiful single-action pedal harp (Fig. C.2). This is pure set decoration, but it illustrates the point mentioned in Chapter I regarding the evolution of the harp in the eighteenth century as an instrument for cultured ladies. The piano and the harp were the proofs of refinement for any aspiring upwardly mobile young lady. I might also mention in passing the various iterations of the Jane Austen novel *Persuasion* (1996/2007) in which the main character plays a harp as a symbol of refinement.

In *Once More, with Feeling*, the harp is a central character in the relationship between a famous orchestral conductor, Yul Brynner, and his lovely companion, Kay Kendall, who happens to be a harpist. In this film, the harp

C.2. Beth March (Eliza Scanlen) has been invited by her neighbor Mr. Laurence (Chris Cooper) to come over and play the piano whenever she wants. Typical nineteenth-century upper-class salon complete with pianoforte and double-action pedal harp. *Little Women*, Columbia Pictures, 2019, screenshot

is actually a musical instrument and not a sign for something else. Kay Kendall serves as Brynner's muse and when she leaves him, his world collapses. Her playing enchants the orchestra's patrons and financial supporters, and it is she who is the power behind Brynner's gruff persona. There's an interesting scene where he destroys her harp in a fit of rage and the prop harp collapses like cardboard. Later, when they reunite, Brynner presents her with an over-the-top gilded model, which she rejects. The harp in this example is an orchestral instrument and Kendall is the muse.

The Argyle Sweater © 2015 Scott Hilburn. Dist. by Andrews McMeel Syndication. Reprinted with permission. All rights reserved.

ACKNOWLEDGMENTS

This work was originally written in partial fulfillment for the Master of Arts degree in Cinema Studies at San Francisco State University. With the exception of those films mentioned above, I'm sure images of harps in have appeared in subsequent movies that I have not seen. I will leave that task to the future film buffs and harp aficionados to bring them to light.

I would like to thank several individuals who helped me with the transformation of this work for publication. Digital technology has finally caught up. I am no longer dealing with video cassettes. DVDs have made the task much easier. I would especially like to thank Jack Decker of the UNC Information Technology Service desk, R.B. House Library, UNC at Chapel Hill, for his cheerful and clear guidance that allowed me to rescue the original manuscript from its format to an updated text version. With his guidance, the ability to capture film images via screenshots allowed the completion of the project. Thanks, Jack. I am indebted to my friend, columnist and film historian, Kevin R. Lewis of Carthage, NC, for his insight and suggestions in realizing this project. Thanks, Kevin. Also, thanks to Russ Covey for his imaginative cover design and to John Havel for assisting with the illustration technology assistance. Lastly, to Julie Allred of BW&A Books for shepherding me throughout the production process.

Finally, I would like to acknowledge my former harp teachers Elizabeth Roth, Linda Booth, and Elizabeth Clark of Charlotte, NC, and my friend Jay Witcher, harp builder of Houlton, ME. And last, but not least, I would like to thank my friend, Lucy Clark Scandrett of Hilton Head, SC, whose performance on her Clark Irish harp so many years ago plucked the strings of my inner harp and awakened me to Hermes. *What the Pluck?*

NOTES

I. ESSENCE OF THE ANCIENT

1. The only other instrument with similar qualities is the glass harmonica. Kenneth R. Piotrowski in "The Harp and the Glass Harmonica" in *The American Harp Journal,* p. 21–22, writes:

Ben Franklin playing a glass harmonica

> The glass harmonica, which is not to be confused with the musical glasses, was invented by American statesman Benjamin Franklin in 1761 and managed within only fifteen years of its creation to rise to an unprecedented popularity shared only by the harp, flute, and piano-forte.
>
> Those fortunate enough to have heard it will never forget its penetratingly soft, disembodied, transparent, and eerie voice, which seems to materialize by means of no earthly agent, floating as though suspended in mid-air, then slowly decaying.
>
> Though the actual timbre is chameleon-like, often resembling the string family or woodwinds, even the celesta in rapid passages, it always possesses the extraordinary unearthly quality for which it was famous. Perhaps for the harpist, its tones would most closely resemble the crystalline and hollow harmonics produced on the harp.
>
> While the harp is incapable of flowing legato lines of a sustained nature, the glass harmonica is not only capable of such executions, it is its essence. Of course, the exact opposite is also true—the glass harmonica is incapable of producing the exquisitely delicate plucking sounds of the harp, at best capable of only muted staccati, which when executed rapidly, produce a shimmering, bell-like effect, again dissimilar to the harp.
>
> The harp has been equated (and appears to have been so since biblical times) with celestial beings; the glass harmonica was, for its brief life, also associated with the heavens. As nearly everyone can tell you, the harp is the instrument of the angels, but the glass harmonica, according to the literature from the second half of the eighteenth century, was considered to be the voices of the angels themselves. Granted, this analogy is hardly scholarly, yet it does clearly symbolize the unique blending abilities of these two instruments. (Piotrowski, AHJ 21–22)

2. For an entertaining look at the history of musical instruments, check out *Toot, Whistle, Plunk and Boom,* Disney's 1953 Academy Award–winning short animation film that depicts the evolution of plucked and bowed stringed instruments with humor and accuracy.

3. Regarding the importance of these instruments in court of ancient Egypt, Roslyn Rensch makes the following observation:

> In the latter part of the nineteenth century Verdi, in the elaborate temple scene of *Aida*, called for the appearance of ancient Egyptian harps on stage. When this opera is performed the chords composed for the temple harps are played on the orchestra's modern pedal harp, usually concealed backstage. While no claim to authenticity can be made for such harp music, the illusion created is highly effective. On seeing *Aida* performed few would deny that the music which seems to emanate from the exotic prop harps on stage adds immeasurably to the grandeur and mysticism of the temple scene. (Rensch 5)

There is an interesting example of the arched Egyptian harp in the 1945 British Technicolor film *Caesar and Cleopatra*, directed by Gabriel Pascal and starring Vivien Leigh and Claude Rains. A scene in Cleopatra's court has her (Vivien Leigh) talking with an advisor about learning to play the harp. The court musician playing the large arched harp is played by the actress Jean Simmons..

Vivien Leigh as Cleopatra with Jean Simmons playing a large Egyptian arched harp. *Caesar and Cleopatra*, directed by Gabriel Pascal, performed by Vivien Leigh and Claude Rains, UK, Eagle-Lion, 1945

The tradition of faking the sound of a prop harp of any description was carried over into cinema with many outrageous examples such as *In the Good Old Summertime*, in which Judy Garland plunks out a love song on a tiny Irish harp with lots of glissandos, or in the 1963 remake of *Cleopatra* as Elizabeth Taylor's court minstrels manage to get their arched harp to sound like a Lyon & Healy concert grand. There is an interesting publicity shot from *Quo Vadis?* showing Nero (Peter Ustinov) standing beside an unidentified studio pedal harpist who may have supplied the glissandos to his cigar-box prop lyre (Fig. 6.9).

4. The most complete study on the subject of Greek stringed instruments is *Stringed Instruments of Ancient Greece* by Martha Maas and Jane M. Snyder.

5. For further discussion of modern ideas concerning the effects of music on learning there are several studies in the *Annals of the New York Academy of Sciences* (vol. 930, June 2001, see bibliography) devoted to "The Biological Foundations of Music." Articles include "Musical Predispositions in Infancy," "Music Cognition Culture and Evolution," "The Brain of Musicians: A Model for Functional and Structural Adaption," and "Music and Nonmusical Abilities."

II. HERMES THE TRICKSTER

1. Two websites: The first relates to the story of Apollo and Hermes and the invention of the lyre (www.talesbeyondbelief.com/myth-stories/hermes-lyre.htm). The second relates to contemporary reconstructions of lyres from Greece together with the story of Apollo and Hermes (https://luthieros.com/product/the-lyre-of-hermes-ancient-greek-lyre-chelys/).

2. The mixture of white and black plumage of the ibis is a reminder of the waning moon. It may be also that the dignified flight and pose of the ibis reminded the Egyptians of the majesty of the moon as it fared across the skies and looked down silently on humankind (Davis 78). In a country in which, as in Egypt, the daily life of the people was largely ordered by reference to the phases of the moon, it was more or less inevitable that the moon god should come to be looked on as the ordering principle of civil and religious life. The easily noted regularity of the moon's phases gave the moon a necessary role in fixing the date of the chief feasts in the temples, and the chief events of the Egyptian civil year (Davis 88).

3. In the introduction to *The Pythagorean Sourcebook and Library,* Fideler also writes:

> The Pythagorean understanding of Number is quite different from the predomi-
> nately quantitative understanding of today. For Pythagoreans, Number is a living,
> qualitative reality which must be approached in an experimental manner. Whereas
> the typical modern usage of number is a sign, to denote a specific quantity or
> amount, the Pythagorean usage is not, in a sense, even a usage at all: Number is not
> something to be *used;* rather, its nature is to be *discovered.* Because Pythagorean
> science possessed a sacred dimension, Number is seen not only as a universal prin-
> ciple, it is a divine principle as well.
>
> The Pythagoreans believed that Number is "the principle, the source and the root
> of all things." The Monad, or Unity, is the principle of Number. In other words, they
> did not see One as a number at all, but as the principle underlying number, which
> is to say that numbers—especially the first ten—may be seen as manifestations of
> diversity in a unified continuum. (Fideler 1987, 21)

> In the Pythagorean and Platonic cosmology, Limit and the Indefinite, Form and Mat-
> ter, are woven together through numerical harmony: their offspring, existing in the
> indefinite receptacle of space, is the phenomenal universe, in which every being is
> composed of universal constants and local variables. Hence, in his Pythagorean cos-
> mology of the *Timaeus,* Plato shows how the fabricator of the cosmos parcels out
> the stuff of the World Soul according to the numerical proportions of the musical
> scale. (Fideler 1987, 24)

> Through the power of Limit, the most formal manifestation of which is Number,
> harmonic nodal points naturally and innately exist on the string, dividing its length
> in halves, thirds, fourths, and so on. The overtone series provides, as it were, the
> architectural foundation of the musical scale, the basic "field" of which is the octave,
> 1:2, or the doubling of the vibrational frequency, which inversely correlates with a
> halving of the string. (Fideler 1987, 25)

> The Pythagoreans divided the study of Number into four branches which may be
> analyzed in the following fashion:

> *Arithmetic* = Number in itself
> *Geometry* = Number in space

Music or Harmonics = Number in time

Astronomy = Number in space and time (Fideler 1987, 34)

We can see the paramount importance of the musical scale and its formation in Pythagorean thought. It suggested for the first time that if a mathematical harmony underlies the realm of tone and music, that Number may account for other phenomena in the cosmic order—for example, planetary motion, which was also thought of being related to the mathematical *harmonia* of the scale, this being the famous "Music of the Spheres." The Pythagoreans were the inheritors of this affinity, and helped to articulate these principles in new, important ways which have profoundly influenced the arts and sciences of Western civilization." (Fideler 1987, 28)

4. In addition to David Fideler's *Jesus Christ, Sun of God: Ancient Cosmology and Early Christian Symbolism*, see Fideler's introduction in *The Pythagorean Sourcebook and Library*, and Christopher Bamford's *Rediscovering Sacred Science*. The foundational texts for Fideler's works are William Sterling's *The Canon*; Bond and Lea's *Gematria: A Preliminary Investigation of the Cabala*; and *Materials for the Study of the Apolistic Gnosis*.

5. Diagram from Fideler, David. *Jesus Christ, Sun of God: Ancient Cosmology and Early Christian Symbolism.* Wheaton, IL: Quest Books, 1993, 215.

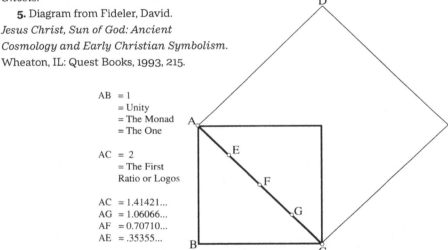

AB = 1
    = Unity
    = The Monad
    = The One

AC = 2
    = The First
    Ratio or Logos

AC = 1.41421...
AG = 1.06066...
AF = 0.70710...
AE = .35355...

Apollo, the Mediator between Unity and Multiplicity

The square with the side AB contains 1 square unit. The square with the side AC contains 2 square units. Length AC is √2, the ideal geometric mean between unity and multiplicity, between 1 and 2. From this value are derived the numbers of Apollo and Hermes, the two Greek personifications of the Logos.

Length		Actual Value	Gematria Value	Greek	English
AC x 1000	=	1414.2	1415	Ὁ ΘΕΟΣ ᾽ΑΠΟΛΛΩΝ	THE GOD APOLLO
AG x 1000	=	1060.6	1061	᾽ΑΠΟΛΛΩΝ	APOLLO
AF x 1000	=	707.1	707	Ὁ ΘΕΟΣ ῾ΕΡΜΗΣ	THE GOD HERMES
AE x 1000	=	353.5	353	῾ΕΡΜΗΣ	HERMES
			354	Ὁ ΘΕΟΣ	THE GOD

III. PLATO'S CAVE AND THE SILVER SCREEN

1. For a detailed discussion on theories of cognitive illusionism and perceptual illusionism, see Gregory Currie's insightful work, *Image and Mind: Film, Philosophy, and Cognitive Science.*

2. Archetypes may be considered the fundamental elements of the conscious mind, hidden in the depths of the psyche. They are systems of readiness for action, and at the same time images and emotions. They are inherited with the brain structure—indeed they are its psychic aspect. Thus, we are driven to the conclusion that a nervous substrate like the sympathetic system, which is absolutely different from the cerebrospinal system in point of origin and function, can evidently produce thoughts and perceptions just as easily as the latter. The sympathetic system could therefore be considered a possible carrier of psychic functions. Dreams then are not produced so much by the sleeping cortex, as in the case of a coma, as by the unsleeping sympathetic system and are therefore of a transcerebral nature (Jacobi 37).

3. A symbol, however, is not a sign. An expression that stands for a known thing always remains a mere sign and is never a symbol. It is, therefore, quite impossible to create a living symbol (i.e., one that is pregnant with meaning) from known associations. Basically, signs and symbols belong to two different planes of reality (Jacobi 80). "[Insofar] as a symbol is a living thing," writes Jung, "it is an expression for something that cannot be characterized in any other better way. The symbol is alive only so long as it is pregnant with meaning. But once its meaning has been born out of it, once the expression is found, which formulates the thing sought, expected, or divined better than the hitherto accepted symbol, the symbol is *dead*, and it becomes a conventional sign. . . . It is, therefore, quite impossible to create a living symbol from known associations" (Jacobi 85). Thus, the symbol is a kind of mediator between the incompatibles of consciousness and the unconscious, between the hidden and the manifest (Jacobi 98). Jung also calls the symbol a psychic *transformer of energy* and points out that it has an eminently "healing" character, that it helps to restore wholeness as well as health (Jacobi 100).

Thus, Jacobi summarizes the conclusions about archetypal psychology as follows:

1. The archetype is a structural factor in the psychic realm of the collective unconscious, a "potential carrier of meaning."
2. Through a suitable constellation—which may be conditioned by individual or collective factors—it receives additional energy.
3. The charge of the archetype is manifested in a kind of magnetic pull on the conscious mind, which, however, is not at first recognized.
4. Attracted by the charge, the light of consciousness falls on the archetype; the archetype enters the actual psychic area, it is *perceived*.
5. When the archetype is "touched by consciousness," it can manifest itself either on the lower biological plane and take form, for instance, as an expression of instinct, or on the higher, spiritual plane as an image or idea. In the latter case the raw material of imagery and meaning are added to it, and the *symbol* is born. The *symbolic guise* in which it becomes visible varies and changes according to the outward and inward circumstances of the individual and the times.
6. The symbol acquires a certain degree of autonomy in its confrontation with the conscious mind.

7. The meaning with which the symbol is "pregnant" compels the conscious mind to come to terms with it.
8. The symbol may:
   a. be brought closer to the conscious mind by understanding and be felt and recognized as in some degree belonging to the ego, but without being wholly fathomed, so that it continues to be "alive" and effective;
   b. be completely fathomed and explored, but it loses its "life" and efficacy and becomes a mere allegory, a "sign," or a conceptually unambiguous content of consciousness;
   c. not be understood at all; it may confront the ego consciousness as an expression of a complex hidden, so to speak, behind it, as a hostile foreign body, split off from it and causing a dissociation in the psyche. It then becomes an *autonomous splinter psyche*, which can make itself felt in the form of "spirits," hallucinations, etc., that is, in all kinds of neurotic and psychotic symptoms (Jacobi 119–121).

Anthony Stevens comments in *Ariadne's Clue: A Guide to the Symbols of Humankind*:

So a distinction has to be made between a thing and its symbolic value. A thing is a thing. Its symbolic value is derived from the meanings and emotions it evokes in us. In other words, a thing becomes a symbol when something has been added to it. This does not alter its nature or its practical significance; it loads it with an increased weight of meaning. (Stevens 7)

According to this view (evolutionary) the mental apparatus is made up of numerous "modules," or archetypes, which have evolved through natural selection to meet specific adaptive problems confronted by our hunter-gatherer ancestors in the past. The modules not only provide the rules to be followed but much of the necessary information as well.

This view, which has now entered the mainstream of behavioral science, is entirely compatible with Jung's later formulation of his archetypal theory, namely, that it is the archetype-as-such which is inherited as an innate predisposition rather than the archetypal images, symbols and patterns of behavior that the archetypes-as-such give rise to. What becomes fixed in the genetic structure is the *predisposition* to develop certain kinds of perception, ideation, or action, and not the actual percepts, ideas, and actions themselves. (Stevens 10)

Any attempt to account for the ubiquitous themes and symbols of the human imagination must, therefore, look beyond the recent Sumerian, Egyptian, Greek, or Roman past to the hunter-gatherer existence for which our psyches were formed. (Stevens 10)

For instead of seeing symbols as a vast array of discrete entities, each with a meaning arbitrarily designated to it by historical tradition, the evolutionary perspective provides a profound and integrated view of the adaptive role that the archetypal symbols have performed in the survival and success of our species. (Stevens 11)

Mircea Eliade maintained that a symbol does not depend for its existence on being understood, known, or even recognized, since it preserves its inherent structure long after it has been forgotten. Thus myths and rituals involving immersion in water (baptism), purification, the deluge (the flood), the submersion of lost continents (Atlantis), the dissolution of the old order and the precipitation of the new (stories of Noah, or of Armageddon and the Apocalypse), all fit together so as to "make up a symbolic system which in a sense pre-existed them all." (Eliade)

They (dreams) may be said to constitute the universal constants of the human psyche. They thus provide copious evidence in support of Jung's hypothesis of a collective unconsciousness, although they do not themselves make this connection. What is more, their findings are in keeping with the overall perspective of evolutionary theory. We are now in a position to carry symbology beyond a Jungian context into the post-Darwinian realm of psychobiology: we can celebrate man as *Homo symbolicum*. (Stevens 20)

The soul, as archetypal psychologist James Hillman has repeatedly pointed out, reveals itself through images (Fideler 1993, 22). This process occurs on both an individual and a transpersonal level, and Jung's insights regarding the archetypes of the collective unconscious have done much to confirm the autonomous nature of the gods, manifest within the soul as patterns of psychic energy. The stumbling block of modern psychology (and many scholars) has been to underestimate the intelligence of the ancients, who, as we shall see, rather than being the unwitting victims of "unconscious projections," developed their knowledge of the gods into a sublime theological, cosmological, and psychological science (Fideler 1993, 22–23). In *Re-Visioning Psychology*, James Hillman writes:

By considering the personified archetypes as Gods, they became more than constitutional propensities and instinctual patterns of behavior, more than ordering structures of the psyche, the ground of its images and vital organs of its functions. They become now recognizable as persons, each with styles of consciousness, or in Jung's language, "typical modes of apprehension." They present themselves each as a guiding spirit with ethical positions, instinctual reactions, modes of thought and speech, and claims upon feeling. Man invents concepts, his tools for grasping, sorting, and taking apart. But he does not invent Gods and daemons. We can replace concepts, even dispense with them altogether, but the archetypal persons are vital organs, and there is no rational substitute for the archetype any more than there is for the cerebellum or the kidneys. They are indispensable to the life of the psyche just as the Gods sustain the universe. Only an [unparalleled] impoverishment of symbolism could enable us to rediscover gods as psychic factors, that is, as archetypes of the unconscious.

But today that is precisely where we do discover the Gods—in the unconscious psyche—and because of this unconsciousness we are unable to distinguish Gods from archetypes, or archetypes from heroes and daemons. Therefore, our descriptions of the archetypes and the classical descriptions of the Gods, heroes, and daemons have to be analogous. The Greeks learned about their Gods through unwritten mythology. We learn about our archetypes through lived psychology. Both can be grasped best as persons. (Hillman 35–36)

Regarding mythology, David Fideler writes:

The transmission and interpretation of myths constituted not only one of the highest arts of the ancient world, but also, as the theological canon of Greek gematria shows, a sacred science as well. It is sadly representative of our time that the word *myth,* in common usage, denotes an untruth, as in the phrase, "It's just a myth." In antiquity, the word *mythos* had just the opposite meaning and denoted a traditional narrative designed to entertain, to educate, and to transmit the very soul and gnosis of the culture. The great scholar-initiates of antiquity such as Plutarch and later Platonists stressed the fact that reality is hierarchical, consisting of different levels. Mythology, it was held, refers to many levels of reality simultaneously. Therefore, if we are to gain insight into the nature of the gods—the divine principles which underlie creation—a particularly instructive approach involves the philosophical interpretation of myth. (Fideler 1993, 23)

VI. THE BARDIC AND ORACULAR TRADITION

1. Blindness was a common characteristic among Irish harpers in the sixteenth and seventeenth centuries mostly as a result of smallpox. Harping can be a tactile art and many harpers were blind, such as Turlough O'Carolan (1670-1783), who lost his sight at age eighteen. He had the great good fortune to be taken in by a patron, Mrs. Ann MacDermott Roe, who had him taught the harp and, when he was a finished pupil, equipped him with a horse and provided him with a servant/guide so that he was launched at the age of twenty-one on his career as a wandering harper. For a detailed study of the bardic tradition in Ireland, see Armstrong 6–23; see also Stewart and Williamson 12–39.

2. "The blending of full-size actors with the tiny leprechauns is achieved entirely by use of forced perspective depth effects," writes Richard Scheib, where the actors playing the large-size people are placed in the foreground and the smaller-size ones at a distance to appear larger/smaller in relation to one another. It's a process that gets around the need for optical patching and the problem of graininess in multiple reprinting's and sloppy matte lines. (The lighting required to make sure the sets were in perspective used up so much electricity it apparently blew out a substation in Burbank when the lights were turned on without warning.) The scenes with hundreds of leprechauns dancing and racing on ponies around giant-size Albert Sharpe is quite an astounding feat when all is considered" (Scheib).

VII. THE NAKED PIANO

1. In an article published in *The Journal of Music Perception and Cognition* and in *The Biological Foundations of Music*, published by the New York Academy of Sciences (see Bibliography) and titled "Music and Testosterone: A New Hypothesis for the Origin and Function of Music," Hajime Fukui studied the testosterone levels in the saliva samples of two separate groups of males and females who had been exposed to a variety of musical styles. His findings indicated there was a significant sex difference in the effects of music. Testosterone decreased under music conditions compared with silence, but not significantly. However, significant sex differences were noted in the effects of music. Testosterone *decreased* in males under all conditions, whereas testosterone *increased* in females under all conditions, revealing that in both sexes the main effects of stimuli were significant (Fukui 449). The conclusions of this study are as follows:

> This study revealed that music affects the testosterone level in both sexes. It is known that the interaction of testosterone with behavior is bidirectional:

testosterone can influence behavior and behavior can influence testosterone levels. Yet the evolutionary function of testosterone changes is unknown. Testosterone has been related to libido, activity level, sensation seeking, and dominance in animals and human beings, and it also plays a part in aggressiveness. Taken together with this evidence, I propose that music has a biological and evolutionary function. However, it not only developed as a signal of courtship, as Darwin remarked, but it also evolved to control human love in a complicated way.

During evolution, the early humans adopted such new reproductive strategies as monogamy, mother-father families, and group living. However, group living intensified all kinds of competition for the resources of reproduction, including food and mates. Human beings needed a system to control these states, which stemmed from sexual, aggressive, and dominant behavior due to excessive testosterone. I suggest that music originated from that need, with its function to control sexual and aggressive behavior. Because testosterone responses to libido differed according to sex, men with lower testosterone levels had low libido, whereas women with higher testosterone levels had higher libidinal capacity, yet they had lower rates of intercourse. Therefore, decreased testosterone levels in males would avoid confrontation and increased testosterone levels in females suppress sexual behavior.

This theory is convincing if we recall that music throughout the world, and even in animal sounds, music and certain sounds function to ease tension or strain, strengthen social bonds, bring pleasure or ecstasy, and bring cohesiveness among people. Music is used empirically and universally in various social situations where stress, tension, and anxiety exist, such as ceremonies, funerals, war, and even banquets. (Fukui 450–451)

2. See "Androgyny and Gay Male Culture: The Recovery of a Native American Tradition for Contemporary Gay Men" in Hopcke's *Jung, Jungians and Homosexuality*. See also "Reclaiming the Exiled Self" by Guy Baldwin and "The Union of the Sames" by Robert Hopcke in *Gay Soul, Finding the Heart of Gay Spirit and Nature*; Mark Thompson's *Gay Body, A Journey Through Shadow To Self* (11–16); and Toby Johnson's *Gay Spirituality: The Role of Gay Identity in the Transformation of Human Consciousness*.

VIII. COMEDY AND FANTASY

1. Several examples of Harpo's antics with the harp appear in the documentary by Davis Leaf and John Scheinfeld, *The Unknown Marx Brothers: A Unique Look at Film's Most Original Comedy Legends*, including a scene with Harpo and Chico as berobed angels playing a duet on a cloud.

IX. CIVILIZATION AND CULTURE

1. King Vidor's 1956 classic version of Tolstoy's *War and Peace* has a similar scene in which Moscow falls to Napoleon. The main characters frantically pack up their townhouse, carrying out all manner of ornate furnishings. The streets are crowded with refugees and cannons are booming in the background. The servants pile wagons high with household valuables. Although there is no harp visible, we know that there had to be one somewhere in all of that stuff!

BIBLIOGRAPHY

Acton, Charles. *Irish Music and Musicians*. Dublin: Eason & Son Ltd., 1978.

Altman, Rick. *Film/Genre*. London: BFI Publishing, 1999.

Armstrong, Robert Bruce. *The Irish and Highland Harps*. New York: Prager Publishers, 1970.

Bamford, Christopher, ed. *Rediscovering Sacred Science*. Edinburgh: Floris Books, 1994.

Benzon, William. *Beethoven's Anvil: Music in Mind and Culture*. New York: Basic Books, 2001.

Bessaraboff, Nicholas. *Ancient European Musical Instruments: An Organological Study of the Musical Instruments in the Leslie Lindsey Mason Collection at the Museum of Fine Arts, Boston*. Cambridge: Harvard University Press, 1941.

Bessy, Maurice. *Erich von Stroheim*. Paris: Pygmalion, 1984.

Bloom, Harold. *Omens of the Millennium: The Gnosis of Angels, Dreams, and Resurrection*. New York: Riverhead Books, 1996.

Bond, Bligh, and Simcox Lea. *Gematria: A Preliminary Investigation of the Cabala*. Wellingborough: Thorsons Publishers Limited, 1977.

Boylan, Patrick. *Thoth. The Hermes of Egypt: A Study of Some Aspects of Theological Thought in Ancient Egypt*. Oxford: Oxford University Press/Sandpiper Books, 1999.

Bragard, Roger, and Dr. Ferdinand J. de Hen. *Musical Instruments in Art and History (Les instruments de musique dans l'art et l'histoire)*. Trans. Bill Hopkins. New York: Viking Press, 1967.

Brophy, Stephen. "*The Loved One* a mixed-up jumble of brilliant parts." *The Tech* 115, no. 47 (06/1995): 9. www.tech.mit.edu/VII5/N47loved.47a.html.

Brown, Norman O. *Hermes the Thief: The Evolution of a Myth*. Madison: University of Wisconsin Press, 1947.

Buchner, Alexander. *Musical Instruments: An Illustrated History*. Trans. by Bofek Vancura. New York: Crown Publishers, 1973.

Bunting, Edward. *The Ancient Music of Ireland*. Dublin: Walton's, 1969.

Cavell, Stanley. *The World Viewed: Reflections on the Ontology of Film*. Cambridge: Harvard University Press, 1979.

Clark, Melville. *How to Play the Harp*. New York: G. Schirmer, Inc., 1932.

Currie, Gregory. *Image and Mind: Film, Philosophy and Cognitive Science*. New York: Cambridge University Press, 1995.

Cuthbert, Shelia Larchet. *The Irish Harp Book: A Tutor and Companion*. Dublin: The Mercer Press, 1975.

Davie, Cedric Thorpe. *Scotland's Music*. Edinburgh: William Blackwood, 1980.

Davis, Erik. *TechGnosis: Myth, Magic, and Mysticism in the Age of Information*. New York: Three Rivers Press, 1998.

East, Katherine. *A King's Treasure: The Sutton Hoo Ship Burial*. Harmondsworth: Kestrel Books, 1982.

Edgerton, Gary R., Michael T. Marsden, and Jack Nachbar, eds. *In the Eye of the Beholder: Cultural Perspectives in Popular Film and Television*. Bowling Green, OH: Bowling Green State Popular Press, 1997.

Eliade, Mircea. *Patterns in Comparative Religion*. Trans. Rosemary Sheed. New York: Sheed & Ward, 1958.

Ellis, Ossian. *The Story of the Harp in Wales*. Cardiff: University of Wales Press, 1980.

Erickson, Glenn. "*The Robe*: A Review." DVD Savant Review. Kleinman.com Inc., 2000. http://www.dvdtalk.com/dvdsavant/s335robe.html.

Erickson, Hal. Synopsis of *Fashions of 1934*. All Movie Guide. Available at https://www.allmovie.com/movie/fashions-of-1934-v16828.

Faivre, Antoine. *The Eternal Hermes: From Greek God to Alchemical Magus*. Trans. Joscelyn Godwin. Grand Rapids, MI: Phanes Press, 1995.

Fideler, David. "Introduction," in Guthrie, Kenneth Sylvan, *The Pythagorean Sourcebook and Library: An Anthology of Ancient Writings Which Relate to Pythagoras and Pythagorean Philosophy*. Grand Rapids, MI: Phanes Press, 1987.

———. *Jesus Christ, Sun of God: Ancient Cosmology and Early Christian Symbolism*. Wheaton, IL: Quest Books, 1993.

Fowden, Garth. *The Egyptian Hermes: An Historical Approach to the Late Pagan Mind*. Princeton, NJ: Princeton University Press, 1993.

Fox, Lilla M. *Instruments of Popular Music: A History of Musical Instruments*. London: Lutterworth Press, 1966.

Freke, Timothy, and Peter Gandy. *The Hermetica: The Lost Wisdom of the Pharaohs*. Tarcher/Putnam, 1999.

Fukui, Hajime. "Music and Testosterone: A New Hypothesis for the Origin and Function of Music." *Annals of the New York Academy of Sciences*. Vol. 930, *The Biological Foundations of Music*. New York: New York Academy of Sciences, 2001. 448–451.

Godwin, Joscelyn. *The Mystery of the Seven Vowels: In Theory and Practice*. Grand Rapids, MI: Phanes Press, 1991.

Geiringer, Karl. *Instruments in the History of Western Music*. New York: Oxford University Press, 1978.

Guthrie, W. K. C. *Orpheus and Greek Religion: A Study of the Orphic Movement*. Princeton, NJ: Princeton University Press, 1993.

Hansen, Jeff. "Plot Summary for *Empire of the Sun* (1987)." Internet Movie Database. https://www.imdb.com/title/tt0092965/.

Hayward, Richard. *The Story of the Irish Harp*. Dublin: Arthur Guinness Son & Co., 1954.

Heymann, Ann. *Secrets of the Gaelic Harp*. Minneapolis, MN: Clairseach Publications, 1988.

Hill, Geoffrey. *Illuminating Shadows: The Mythic Power of Film*. Boston, MA: Shambhala Publications, Inc., 1992.

Hillman, James. *Re-Visioning Psychology*. New York: Harper & Row, 1976.

Hopcke, Robert H. *Jung, Jungians, and Homosexuality*. Boston, MA: Shambhala Publications, Inc., 1989.

Huron, David. "Is Music an Evolutionary Adaptation?" *Annals of the New York Academy of Sciences*. Vol. 930, *The Biological Foundations of Music*. New York: New York Academy of Sciences, 2001.

Jacobi, Jolande. *Complex/Archetype/Symbol in the Psychology of C. G. Jung*. Princeton, NJ: Princeton University Press, 1959.

Jarvie, Ian. *Philosophy of the Film: Epistemology, Ontology, Aesthetics*. New York: Routledge & Kegan Paul, 1987.

Johnson, Toby. *Gay Spirituality: The Role of Gay Identity in the Transformation of Human Consciousness*. Los Angeles, CA: Alyson Books, 2000.

Jung, C. G. *The Archetypes and the Collective Unconscious*. Bollingen Series XX. Second Edition. Princeton, NJ: Princeton University Press, 1968.

Kerenyi, Karl. *Hermes: Guide of Souls*. Trans. Murray Stein. Woodstock, CT: Spring Publications, Inc., 1996.

Kinnaird, Alison. *The Harp Key*. Shillinghill, Temple, Midlothian, Scotland: Kinmor Music, 1986.

Koester, Helmut. *Introduction to the New Testament, Volume 1: History, Culture, and Religion of the Hellenistic Age*. Second Edition. New York: Walter de Gruyer, 1995.

Lea, Simcox, and Bligh Bond. *Materials for the Study of the Apostolic Gnosis*. Wellingborough: Thorson's Publishers Limited, 1919.

Maas, Martha and Jane McIntosh Snyder. *Stringed Instruments of Ancient Greece*. New Haven, CT: Yale University Press, 1989.

Marcuse, Sibyl. *A Survey of Musical Instruments*. New York: Harper & Row, 1975.

Marx, Harpo, and Rowland Barber. *Harpo Speaks!* New York: Bernard Geis Publishers, 1962.

McLuhan, Marshall. *Understanding: The Extensions of Man*. New York: McGraw-Hill, 1964.

Merry, Eleanor C. *The Flaming Door*. Edinburgh: Floris Books, 1983.

Miles, Dillwyn. *The Royal National Eisteddfod of Wales*. Swansea: Christopher Davies, 1978.

Milligan, Samuel, "The Oracular Nature of the Early Celtic Harp." *The American Harp Journal*. 1, no. 1 (Spring 1967): 12–18.

Nichols, Ross. *The Book of Druidry: History, Sites, Wisdom*. London: The Aquarian Press, 1990.

Pike, Bob, and Dave Martin. *The Genius of Busby Berkeley*. Reseda, CA: CFS Books, 1973.

Piotrowski, Kenneth R. "The Harp and the Glass Harmonica." *The American Harp Journal* 11, no. 3 (Summer 1988).

Powell, Barry B. *Classical Myth*. Second Edition. Upper Saddle River, New Jersey: Prentice Hall, 1998.

Remnant, Mary. *Musical Instruments: An Illustrated History from Antiquity to the Present*. Portland, OR: Amadeus Press, 1989.

Rensch, Roslyn. *Harps and Harpists*. Bloomington: Indiana University Press, 1989.

Rhodes, Steve. Review of *Small Time Crooks*. *rec. arts. movies. reviews* newsgroup. Available at https://www.cinafilm.com/movies/small-time-crooks-2000/reviews/981728-although-has-few-nice-laughs-movie-never-rises-above-forgettable/.

Rimmer, Joan. *The Irish Harp, Cláirseach na hÉireann.* Dublin and Cork: The Mercier Press, 1969.

Rowley, Gill, ed. *The Book of Music.* London: New Burlington Books, 1977.

Sachs, Curt. *The History of Musical Instruments.* New York: W. W. Norton & Co., 1940.

Scheib, Richard. *"Darby O'Gill and the Little People,* a Review." 1991. https://www .moriareviews.com/fantasy/darby-ogill-and-the-little-people-1959.htm.

Schroeder-Sheker, Therese. "The Alchemical Harp of Mechtild of Hackeborn." *Alexandria* 2 (1993): 113-26.

Schwartz, Dennis. Review of *Amistad* (1997). *Ozus's World Movie Reviews.* February 17, 1999. https://dennisschwartzreviews.com/amistad/.

———. Review of *Blood of a Poet (Le sang d'un poete)* (1930). *Ozus's World Movie Reviews.* November 25, 1999. https://dennisschwartzreviews.com/bloodofapoet/.

———. Review of *Quo Vadis?* (1951). *Ozus's World Movie Reviews.* May 11, 2000. https://dennisschwartzreviews.com/quovadis/.

Schwartz, H. W. *The Story of Musical Instruments: From Shepherd's Pipe to Symphony.* New York: Doubleday, Doran & Co., Inc., 1938.

Sheehy, Jeanne. *The Rediscovery of Ireland's Past: The Celtic Revival 1830-1930.* London: Thames and Hudson, 1980.

Spence, Lewis. *An Encyclopedia of Occultism: A Compendium of Information on the Occult Sciences, Occult Personalities, Psychic Science, Magic, Demonology, Spiritism, Mysticism and Metaphysics.* New Hyde Park: University Books, 1960.

Steinke, Gary Lee. *An Analysis of the Dance Sequences in Busby Berkeley's Films: "Forty Second Street," "Footlight Parade," and "Gold Diggers of 1935."* Diss., University of Michigan, 1979.

Stevens, Anthony. *Ariadne's Clue: A Guide to the Symbols of Humankind.* Princeton, NJ: Princeton University Press, 1998.

Stewart, R. J., and Robin Williamson. *Celtic Bards, Celtic Druids.* London: Blandford, 1996.

Stirling, William. *The Canon: An Exposition of the Pagan Mystery Perpetuated in the Cabala as the Rule of All the Arts.* London: The Garnstone Press Limited, 1974.

Stunzi, Lilly. *Musical Instruments of the Western World.* New York: McGraw-Hill, 1966.

Thompson, Mark. *Gay Body: A Journey through Shadow to Self.* New York: St. Martin's Press, 1999.

Thompson, Mark, ed. *Gay Soul: Finding the Heart of Gay Spirit and Nature with Sixteen Writers, Healers, Teachers, and Visionaries.* San Francisco, CA: Harper-Collins, 1995.

Yates, Frances A. *Giordano Bruno and the Hermetic Tradition.* Chicago: University of Chicago Press, 1964.

Yeats, Grainne. *The Belfast Harper's Festival 1792.* Dublin: Gael-Linn, 1980.

Zatorre, Robert J. and Isabelle Peretz, eds. *Annals of the New York Academy of Sciences.* Vol. 930, *The Biological Foundations of Music.* New York: New York Academy of Sciences, 2001.

Zimmerman, Paul D., and Burt Goldblat. *The Marx Brothers at the Movies.* New York: G. P. Putnam's Sons, 1968.

Zingel, Hans J. *King David's Harp.* Köln: Musikverlage Hans Gerig, 1968.

FILMOGRAPHY

Absent-Minded Professor, The. Directed by Robert Stevenson. Performed by Fred MacMurray, Nancy Olsen, Keenan Wynn, and Tommy Kirk. Disney, 1961. Videocassette, Disney Home Video, 1986.

Amistad. Directed by Steven Spielberg. Performed by Morgan Freeman, Nigel Hawthorne, Anthony Hopkins, Djimon Hounsou, Kevin Jackson, Matthew McConaughey, Tomas Milian, and Anna Paquin. DreamWorks, 1997. Videocassette, DreamWorks, 1998.

Angel Who Pawned Her Harp, The. Directed by Alan Bromly. Performed by Diane Cilento and Felix Alymer. Prod. Group 3, 1954. VCI-DVD.

Aristocats, The. Directed by Wolfgang Reitherman. Disney, 1970. Videocassette, Disney Home Video, 1986.

Bananas. Directed by Woody Allen. Performed by Woody Allen and Louise Lasser. Jack Rollins-Charles Joffe production, 1971. DVD, MGM, 2000.

Bedazzled. Directed by Harold Ramis. Performed by Brendan Fraser, Francis O'Connor, Elizabeth Hurley, and Orlando Jones. Fox, 2000. Videocassette, Fox Home Video, 2001.

Bishop's Wife, The. Directed by Henry Koster. Performed by Cary Grant, Loretta Young, and David Niven. 1947. DVD, Warner Brothers, 2013.

Blood of a Poet. Directed by Jean Cocteau. Performed by Lee Miller, Enrico Rivero, and Jean Desbordes. Janus Films, Inc., 1930. Videocassette, Public Media Incorporated, 1980.

Brazil. Directed by Terry Gilliam. Performed by Jim Broadbent, Ray Cooper, Robert DeNiro, Kim Greist, Katherine Helmond, Ian Holm, Michael Palin, Jonathan Pryce, and Ian Richardson. Universal, 1985. Videocassette, MCA Home Video, 1986.

Bugsy Malone. Directed by Alan Parker. Performed by Scott Baio, Dexter Fletcher, Jodie Foster, Michael Jackson, John Lee, and John Williams. Paramount, 1976. Videocassette, Paramount Home Video, 1981.

Cleopatra. Directed by Cecil B. DeMille. Performed by Claudette Colbert, Henry Wilcoxon, and Warren Williams. Universal, 1934. Videocassette, MCA Home Video, 1995.

Cleopatra. Directed by Joseph L. Mankiewicz. Performed by Elizabeth Taylor, Richard Burton, Rex Harrison, Pamela Brown, Hume Cronyn, and Roddy McDowell. Twentieth Century-Fox, 1963. Videocassette, Fox Video, 1992.

Dangerous Liaisons. Directed by Stephen Frears. Performed by Peter Capaldi, Glenn Close, Swoosie Kurtz, John Malkovich, Michelle Pfeiffer, Keanu Reeves, and Uma Thurman. Warner Brothers, 1988. Videocassette, Warner Home Video, 1993.

Darby O'Gill and the Little People. Directed by Robert Stevenson. Performed by Albert Sharpe, Janet Munro, Sean Connery, and Walter Fitzgerald. Disney, 1959. Videocassette, Buena Vista Home Video, 1992.

David and Goliath. Directed by Ferdinando Baldi. Performed by Pierre Cressoy, Edward Hilton, Ivo Payer, and Orson Welles. Allied Artists, 1961. Videocassette, Sinister Cinema, 1994.

Day at the Races, A. Directed by Sam Wood. Performed by Frankie Darro, Margaret Dumot, Allan Jones, Chico Marx, Groucho Marx, Harpo Marx, Jack Norton, Maureen O'Sullivan, and Sig Rumann. MGM, 1937. Videocassette, MGM/UA/Turner, 1988.

Egyptian, The. Directed by Michael Curtiz. Performed by Edmund Purdom, Jean Simmons, Peter Ustinov, Michael Wilding, Gene Tierney, and Victor Mature. Twentieth Century-Fox, 1954. Videocassette, Fox Video, 1992.

Empire of the Sun. Directed by Steven Spielberg. Performed by Christian Bale, John Malkovich, and Miranda Richardson. Warner Bros., 1987. Videocassette, Warner Home Video, 1988.

Fantasia. Directed by James Algar. Performed by Leopold Stokowski. Disney, 1940. Videocassette, Buena Vista Home Video, 2000.

Fashions of 1934. Directed by William Dieterle. Musical direction by Busby Berkeley. Performed by William Powell, Betty Davis, Jane Darwell, and Arthur Treacher. Warner Brothers, 1934. Warner Archive, 2011.

For Heaven's Sake. Directed by George Seaton. Performed by Clifton Webb and Joan Bennett. Twentieth Century-Fox, 1950. Videocassette, Fox Home Video, 2012.

Gone with the Wind. Directed by Victor Fleming. Performed by Vivien Leigh, Clark Gable, Leslie Howard, Olivia de Havilland, and Hattie McDaniel. MGM, 1939. Videocassette, MGM Home Entertainment/Turner, 1998.

Harry Potter and the Sorcerer's Stone. Directed by Chris Columbus. Performed by Daniel Radcliffe, Rupert Grint, Emma Watson, Robbie Coltrane, and Richard Harris. Warner Bros., 2001.

High Anxiety. Directed by Mel Brooks. Performed by Madeline Kahn, Mel Brooks, Harry Kramer, and Cloris Leachman. Twentieth Century-Fox, 1978. Videocassette, Magenta Video/Fox, 1981.

How the West Was Won. Directed by John Ford, Henry Hathaway, and George Marshall. Performed by John Wayne, Henry Fonda, Debbie Reynolds, James Stewart, Carroll Baker, Gregory Peck, Lee J. Cobb, and George Peppard. MGM, 1962. Videocassette, MGA Home Video/Turner, 1994.

In the Good Old Summertime. Directed by Robert Z. Leonard. Performed by Spring Byington, Judy Garland, Van Johnson, Buster Keaton, and S. Z. Sakall. Loew's, Inc., 1949. Videocassette, MGM/UA/Turner, 1986.

Little Women. Directed by Greta Gerwig. Performed by Saoirse Ronan, Emma Watson, Florence Pugh, Eliza Scanlen, Laura Dern, Chris Cooper, and Timothée Chalamet. Columbia Pictures, 2019.

Loved One, The. Directed by Tony Richardson. Performed by Robert Morse, Robert Morley, Jonathan Winters, and Anjanette Comer. MGM, 1965. Videocassette, MGM/UA/Turner, 1990.

Magic Christian, The. Directed by Joseph McGrath. Performed by Peter Sellers, Ringo

Starr, Christopher Lee, Spike Milligan, Raquel Welch, and Yul Brynner. Republic Pictures, 1970. Videocassette, Republic Pictures Home Video, 1985.

Mickey and the Beanstalk. Directed by Hamilton Luske and Bill Roberts. Disney, 1947. Videocassette, Disney Mini Classic, Buena Vista Home Video, 2009.

Once More, with Feeling. Directed by Stanley Doren. Performed by Yul Brynner, Kay Kendall, and Geoffrey Toone. Columbia Pictures, 1960.

Quo Vadis? Directed by Mervyn LeRoy. Performed by Robert Taylor, Deborah Kerr, Leo Genn, Peter Ustinov, Patricia Laffer, Finlay Currie, and Buddy Baer. Loew's, Inc., 1951. Videocassette, MGM Home Video, 1986.

Robe, The. Directed by Henry Koster. Performed by Richard Burton, Jean Simmons, Jay Robinson, Victor Mature, and Michael Pennie. Twentieth Century-Fox, 1953. Videocassette, CBS/Fox Video, 1987.

Small Time Crooks. Directed by Woody Allen. Performed by Woody Allen, Tracey Ullman, Hugh Grant, Jon Lovitz, Elaine May, and Michael Rapaport. DreamWorks Pictures, 2000. Videocassette, DreamWorks Home Video, 2000.

Strike Up the Band. Directed by Busby Berkeley. Performed by Judy Garland, Mickey Rooney, Enid Bennett, Helen Eddy, Larry Nunn, William Tracy, and Paul Whitman. Loew's, Inc., 1940. Videocassette, MGM/UA/Turner, 1991.

Tall Blond Man with One Black Shoe, The (Le grand blond avec une chaussure noire). Directed by Yves Robert. Performed by Pierre Richard, Jean Rochefort, and Mireille Darc. Gaumont International/Productions de la Gueville/Madeleine Films, 1973. Videocassette, Connoisseur Video Collection, 1990.

Toot, Whistle, Plunk and Boom. Directed by Ward Kimball and Charles Nichols. Disney, 1953. Videocassette, Disney Home Video, Limited Gold Edition, 1984.

Unfaithfully Yours. Directed by Preston Sturges. Performed by Rex Harrison, Linda Darnell, Rudy Vallee, Edgar Kennedy, and Lionel Stander. Twentieth Century-Fox, 1948. Videocassette, CBS/Fox Video, 1984.

Unknown Marx Brothers, The: A Unique Look at Film's Most Original Comedy Legends. Directed by Davis Leaf and John Scheinfeld. Narrated by Leslie Nielsen. Crew Neck Productions, 1993. Videocassette, Winstar Home Entertainment, 1997.

Wedding March, The. Directed by Erich von Stroheim. Performed by Fay Wray, Zasu Pitts, George Fawcett, and Erich von Stroheim. Paramount Famous Lasky Corp, 1928. Videocassette, Paramount Home Video, 1987.

INDEX

Note: Page numbers in italics refer to
screenshots, other illustrations, and
their captions.

Craftine, 77

crossbar of lyre, 8

cruit (chrotta), 8

crwth (bowed lyre), 24, 25

culture and civilization, harp and, 2,
113–22

Cummings, Robert, in *For Heaven's Sake*
(1950), 65

cythara angelica, 26, 33, 36

Dali, Salvador, 106

Dangerous Liaisons (1988), 90, 100, *101*

Darby O'Gill and the Little People (1959),
83–87, *85, 86*

Dark Ages, 8

David, King, 2, *25*, 34, 36, 60–61, *61*; harp
of, 10, 59–60

Davis, Bette, in *Fashions of 1934*, 94–95

Davis, Erik, 41, 42, 43, 48, 53, 131n2

Day at the Races, A (1937), 106; harp as
soul of music in, 3, *4, 5*

death, funerals, and grave goods, 7–8, *11*,
12

Dieterle, William, as director of *Fashions
of 1934*, 94

Dilling, Mildred, 106

Diogenes of Oinomaos, 20

Dionysius of Thrace, 18

Dionysus, 17

Disney's *Fantasia* (1948), 5

divination, 77–78

Donald Duck, *93*, 94

Doren, Stanley, as producer of *Once
More, with Feeling* (1960), 124

double-string harp, 26. See also *arpa
doppia*

Douglas, Lloyd, 79

druidism, druids, 77–78

drums, 8

Durer, Albrecht, 36

Egypt, 2, 26, 131n2; arched harp in, *11*,
11–12; harps in ancient, 7–8, 9, *9, 11*, 11–12

Egyptian harp, 130n3

Eliade, Mircea, 134–35n3

Elizabeth I, Queen of England, 30, *30*, 92

Empire of the Sun (1987), *115*, 115–17, *116*

England, 8, 25–26, 29, 31, 55, 62, 90

Epicurus, 22

Erard, Pierre, 38

Erard, Sebastian, 38

Erickson, Glenn, 78–79

Erickson, Hal, 94

Erin (Pearce and Sharpe statue, 1889),
32

Eros, 17

ethos, 12

etymology of "harp," 6

Europe, 12, 24. *See also names of
individual countries of*

European harp, 33, 36

Eusebius of Caesarea, 18

Ezekiel, 10

Fantasia (Disney, 1948), 5

Fashions of 1934 (1934), 94–95, *95*;
female human-harps in, 57

feminization of harp, 89–104. *See also*
women

Fideler, David, 14–15, 49–50, 51–52,
131–32n3, 132n5, 135–36n3

film and movies: *The Absent-Minded
Professor* (1961), 107–8, *108*; *Amadeus*
(1984), 18; *Amistad* (1997), 57, 117–19,
118; *The Angel Who Pawned Her
Harp* (1954), *66*, 66–67; animated, 5,
71–72, *72*, 92, *93*, 94, 105, 112, 129n2;
The Aristocats, (1970), 94; *Bananas*
(1971), 108–10, *109*; *Bedazzled* (2000),
57, 100–103, *102*; *Ben-Hur* (1959), 83;
The Bishop's Wife (1947), 2, 56–57,
63–64, *64*; *Bugsy Malone* (1976), 112,
112; *Caesar and Cleopatra* (1945),
130n3, *130n3*; *Cleopatra* (1963),
130n3; criticism and critics of, 53,
73, 78, 80; *Dangerous Liaisons*
(1988), 90, 100, *101*; *Darby O'Gill
and the Little People* (1959), 83–87,
85, 86; *A Day at the Races* (1937), 3,
4, 5, 106; *Empire of the Sun* (1987),
115, 115–17, *116*; *Fantasia* (Disney,
1948), 5; *Fashions of 1934* (1934), 57,
94–95, *95*; *For Heaven's Sake* (1950),
64–65, *65*; *Gladiator* (2000), 83;

Hayward, Richard, 6, 29, 30, 31
Heaven Can Wait (1943), 2
heavenly instrument, harp as, 2, 113. *See also* angels and harps
Hebrews, 10
Hellenistic Greece, 21
hemp string, 15–16
Henry VIII, King of Britain, 30
Hermes, 15, 18, *42*, 60, 76; Apollo and, 41–42; as boundary-crosser, 78, 103; lyre invented by, 1, 2, 41, 103; magical power of, 43, 67; as patron of cinema, 53–54; as patron of gay culture, 92, 104; as trickster, 1, *2*, 41–52, 103, 104
Herodotus, 19
High Anxiety (1981), 108, *109*
Hill, Geoffrey, 1, 54, 55, 57
Hillman, James, 135n3
history of earliest music, 6–12
Hopke, Robert H., 103, 104
Hopkins, Anthony, in *Amistad* (1997), 117
Horace, 22
Hortense, Queen of Holland, 91
Hounsou, Dijmon, in *Amistad* (1997), 117
Howard, Henry, 31
How the West Was Won (1962), *98*, 98–99
Hudson, Edward, 32
human voice, 75
Hurley, Elizabeth, in *Bedazzled* (2000), 101–3
Huron, David, 8, 13
Hyde-White, Wilfrid, in *The Magic Christian* (1969), 119
hydraulos (water organ), 22–23, *23*
Hyksos, 10

ideas, Plato on, 1
idiophones, 8
In the Good Old Summertime (1949), 95–96, *96*, 130n3
invention of harp, mythological, 32
Ireland: harp in, 26–33, 39; personified as Erin, *32*
Irish harp, 6, 26, *27*; as heraldic device, 29–30, *30*, 95, *96*; history of, 27–33; as national emblem, 32

Irish harpers and harpists, 27, 28, 29, 31, 136n1; tradition of, 39. *See also* bard, bards
Isiah, 10
Isidore, Bishop of Seville, 34
Islam, 63

"Jack and the Beanstalk," 92
Jacobi, Jolande, 55–56, 133–134n3
James I, King of Britain, 30, *30*
Jarvie, Ian, 54, *54*
John of Salisbury, 29
Johnson, Van, in *In the Good Old Summertime* (1949), 95–96, *96*
jongleurs, 24, 34
Josephine, Empress of France, 91
Judaism, 10, 21, 63
Jung, Carl, archetypal theory of, 1, 122, 133–35n3
Juvenal, 22

Kassites, 10
Kavanaugh, H. T., 83
Kendall, Kay, in *Once More, with Feeling* (1960), 124–25
Kerr, Deborah, in *Quo Vadis?*, 80
keyboard instruments, 6, 18. *See also* piano, pianos
kinnor (box lyre), 10–11, *79*, 80
kithara, cithara, 8, *9*, 12–13, 15–17, *17*, 22, 23; gender and, 82, 90; players of, *17*, 77; strings of, 19, 22. *See also* lyre
kitharistes (lyre teacher), 13
kitharoedoi, 77
Koester, Helmut, 21
Ktesibios, 23

Lamont harp, *31*
Larson, Gary, "Welcome to Hell," 59
Laughton, Gayle, in *The Bishop's Wife*, 63
Lee, Christopher, in *The Magic Christian* (1969), 119
Le grand blonde avec une chaussure noire (1973), 111–12
Leigh, Vivien: in *Caesar and Cleopatra* (1945), 130n3, *130n3*; in *Gone With the Wind* (1939), 114, *114*

Niven, David, in *The Bishop's Wife* (1947), 64
notes, musical, 6, 16

oak, 77-78
O'Carolan, Turlough, 136n1
O'Connor, Frances, in *Bedazzled* (2000), 101-3
Once More, with Feeling (1960), 124-25
O'Neill, Arthur, *28*
O'Neill harp, *28*
oracular tradition, 75-88
organ, pipe, 5, 6, 33, 34, *34*
organ, pneumatic, 23-24
organ, water, 22-23, *23*
Orpheus, 12, 17; as magical musician, *48*, 48-49; metamorphosed into King David, 35, 60

Pandora, 43
panpipes (*syrinx*), 13, 23, 34
Pascal, Gabriel, as director of *Caesar and Cleopatra* (1945), 130n3
Peck, Gregory, in *How the West Was Won* (1962), *98*, 98-99
pedal mechanism, 38
pektis, 19, 20, 82; as woman's instrument, 19-20, 90
Persuasion (1996/2007), 124
Phoenicians, 10
phorminx, *20*
piano, pianos, 3, *4*, 6
Pike, Bob, 94
Pindar, 19
Plato, 1, 12, 17, 18, 131n3; on music and instruments, 13, 18, 19; on *trigonon*, 15, 21
Plato's Cave, 53-57, 124
Playboy magazine, *7*
plectrum, 15, 19
Pliny, 78
plucking, 6, 8, 15, 19, 20, 24, 27, 35, 38, 80, 83, 96, 110
Plutarch, 47
Poe, Edgar Allan, 101
poetry, 17-18, 77, 78

politics and harp, 31-32
polyphonic music, 24
popular culture, harps in, 59
Porphyry, 18
Porphyry the Neoplatonist, 18
Powell, Barry, 75-76
Powell, William, in *Fashions of 1934*, 94-95
Pretorius, Michael, 26
primitive music, 75
prop harps and lyres, 130n3
proportion, Greeks and, 2
psalterion, 12, 19
purity of harp's tonal quality, 3, 5
Pythagoras, 12
Pythagoreans, 2, 5, 13-15, 49; archetypal nature of harp and, 50-52

Quo Vadis? (1951), 80-83, *81*, *82*, *83*, 130n3

Rachmaninov, Segei, 3
Rains, Claude, in *Caesar and Cleopatra* (1945), 130n3
Ramesses III's tomb, 7-8, *11*, 12
Reeves, Keanu, in *Dangerous Liaisons*, 90, 100
religion, 55, 69; Egyptian, 45, 48, 49, 131n2; Greek, 21, 44, 45, 48-49; music and, 22, 75
Remnant, Mary, 36, 38
Rensch, Roslyn, 12, 20, 27, 38, 61, 91
Reynolds, Debbie, in *How the West Was Won* (1962), 98-99
Rhodes, Steve, 120
rhythm, musical, 6
Richard, Pierre, in *The Tall Blonde Man with One Black Shoe* (1973), 111
Richardson, Miranda, in *Empire of the Sun* (1987), 117
Rimmer, Joan, 23-24, 26-27, 28-29, 31
Robe, The (1953), 78-80, *79*
Rome, Romans, 2; Empire of, 21, 24; Greece conquered by, 21, 22; musical instruments of, 18, 22
Rooney, Mickey, in *Strike Up the Band* (1940), 99-100

transformation, harp as agent of, 3, 5

Tree of Jesse, 61

triangular harp, *26*

trickster archetype: Harpo Marx as, 1, 2;
  Hermes as, 1, 2, 41–52, 103, 104

trigonon, 12, *13*, 15, 18; in Sophocles,
  20–21; women and, 19, 90. *See also*
  angled harps

Trinity College, 27

triple goddess, 78

tuning, 15, 37

Tutilo of St. Gallen, 24

Twenty-Four Elders, 61–62, *62*

tympanum, 15

Ullman, Tracey, in *Small Time Crooks*
  (2000), 119–22

Unfaithfully Yours (1948), *110*, 110–11

USA Weekend, 89

Ustinov, Peter, in *Quo Vadis?* (1951),
  80–82

Valley of the Kings, 7–8

Venantius Fortunatus, 25

vertical harps, 26

viol, 8, 25

violin, 1, 6, 8, *98*, 99, 111, *111*

visuality of harp, 105, 122

von Stronheim, Erich, in *The Wedding
  March* (1928), 96–97

Wales, 24, 38

War and Peace (1956), 137n1

water organ (*hydraulos*), 22–23, *23*

Webb, Clifton, in *For Heaven's Sake*
  (1950), 64–65

Wedding March, The (1928), 96–97, *97*

"Welcome to Hell" (Larson cartoon,
  1986), *58*

Wendel, Tim, *88*, 89

West Highland harp, *36*

willow, 77–78

wind instruments, 8, 22

women, 19–20, 22; harp and, 12, 78, 82,
  90, 92, *92*, 94, 95. *See also* feminization of harp

Wray, Fay, in *The Wedding March* (1928),
  96–97, *97*

xylophones, 8

Yeats, William Butler, 55

yoke, 8, 15, 24

Young, Loretta, in *The Bishop's Wife*
  (1947), 63–64

You've Got Mail (1998), 95

Zimmerman, Paul D., 106

Zingel, Hans, 60–61

zither, 8–9

Zoroastrianism, 63

ABOUT THE AUTHOR

F. Marion Redd is a graduate of the University of North Carolina at Chapel Hill with an AB in History and Radio, Television and Motion Pictures. He also has his MA in Cinema Studies from San Francisco State University and his MA from the California Institute of Integral Studies in Philosophy, Cosmology and Consciousness. For several years, he served as treasurer of the Charlotte, NC, chapter of the American Harp Society and was an original southeastern director for the Society of Folk Harpers and Craftsmen.

He resides in Hillsborough, NC, and still plays his wire-strung Witcher Celtic harp and a new Lyon & Healy Ogden lever harp, which replaced an earlier Salvi Daphne pedal harp.